Angel Magic

all about angels and how to bring
their magic into your life

Angel Magic

all about angels and how to bring
their magic into your life

Margaret Neylon

element

Element
An Imprint of HarperCollins*Publishers*
77–85 Fulham Palace Road,
Hammersmith, London W6 8JB

The website address is: www.thorsonselement.com

and *Element* are trademarks of
HarperCollins*Publishers* Limited

First published by Thorsons, an imprint of HarperCollins*Publishers* 2001
This edition published by Element 2002

12 11

© Margaret Neylon 2001

Margaret Neylon asserts the moral right
to be identified as the author of this work

ISBN-13   978-0-00-712133-5
ISBN-10   0-00-712133-4

A catalogue record of this book is
available from the British Library

Printed and bound in Great Britain by
Martins the Printers Ltd, Berwick upon Tweed

Contents

Introduction

Before we begin to look at how to connect with our angels and bring angelic magic into our lives, we need to understand just what an angel is. The word 'angel' comes from the Greek 'angelos' which means 'messenger from God'. Practically every belief system or religion, whether originating in the West or the East, includes beings – called angels, peri, fravashi or devas – who are sent by God to undertake special missions with us humans here on Earth. The dictionary tells us that angels are 'immaterial beings, pure spirits, intermediaries between man and God, who are

always at our side and instructed to guard and guide us.' It is because they are the intermediaries between ourselves and the Source (God) that they can work magic with us. They are not New Age creations, nor working only in California, USA or Byron Bay, New South Wales, but they have been a part of mankind's belief system for more than 7,000 years. You don't have to be mad to have an angel, and neither do you have to be perfect, nor even religious, for angels were created by God to connect with mankind, while religions were made by mankind to connect with God.

As Saint Thomas Aquinas said way back in the 13th century: 'Angels transcend every religion, every philosophy, every creed. In fact angels have no religion as we know it; their existence precedes every religious system that has ever existed on earth.' Three hundred years later the French religious leader and theologian John Calvin wrote: 'The angels are the dispensers and administers of the divine beneficence toward us; they regard our safety, undertake our defense, direct our ways, and exercise a constant solicitude that no evil befalls us.' But, as Saint Thomas Aquinas pointed out: 'A man does not always choose what his guardian angel intends!'

Angels were created by God to connect with mankind, while religions were made by mankind to connect with God.

What Is Magic?

Often the very word 'magic' can conjure up fearful images of darkness, fire, brimstone, hell, and anything else which portrays something sinister. This is because we tend not to understand what magic is and where it comes from. Just as the 'bogie man' was introduced to people of my generation to keep us close to home, countless generations have woven stories of ogres and werewolves, vampires, warlocks and witches into Cecil B. De Mille-like cine-dramas in order to keep us in awe of the storyteller.

There is nothing like a little knowledge to empower oneself, so let's look at the meaning of some of the words which are connected with making magic in order to understand more about it.

Firstly, the word 'magic'. Christians will be familiar with the word 'magi' from the coming of the three magi to the infant Jesus

in Bethlehem. (They are also known as the 'three wise men'.) Magi is the plural of the word 'magos', a Persian/Greek word meaning 'sorcerer' – someone who goes to the 'source' in order to empower things to happen. 'Magos' became 'magikos' as an adjective, which later became the Latin 'magica', and we now know it as 'magic' which is what a 'magician' uses to make things happen that we wonder at. The Latin 'mirari' means 'to wonder at' and we get the word 'miracle' from 'miraculum', 'something to be wondered at'. The word 'spell' comes from the French word 'espeler' which translates as 'to read out' or to 'name the letters of a word'. It has been known for many thousands of years that every word, especially when written, has enormous power. The very earliest written documents from China still exist in almost pristine condition simply because those people knew the importance of their written text. In most of the major religions only the ministers would read the holy books, and such knowledge was banned from women, in particular, for many centuries. As the saying goes, 'knowledge is power'!

So now we know the background to the words 'magic', 'magician', 'miracle' and 'spell' and therefore realize they are

merely words. They have no power unless we give them power ourselves, and there is certainly no negativity involved. As 'knowledge is power' most of the world's powerful bodies have done their utmost to keep the masses in ignorance in order that they be disempowered and therefore obedient through fear of the unknown. In some countries only the wealthy can become knowledgeable through academia, but everyone has their own ability to become self-empowered and it is virtually free of cost. I did myself, with angelic help. You, too, can empower yourself with the help of your angels, and this is what Angel Magic is all about.

Is Magic Dangerous?

Your next question may be 'But isn't magic dangerous?' The simple answer to that is 'No it is not!' I believe we are spirits who have decided to have an earthly experience in order to learn certain lessons on the pathway to spiritual and personal development. I believe our spirits are enveloped by our physical body and our mind is governed by our ego. However, no

matter how fearful our ego may be, we always have our spiritual connection which is fearless. Why should it be fearful when it is connected to God and the angels? But it's as though the human part of us has forgotten that we have this source of knowledge through our spirit, and so we need to learn it again here on Earth. All the tuition we need is readily available through our spirit. It's what we call 'intuition' because it comes from within. Our angels are here to help us on our pathway through 'the University of Life', just as a teacher helps us at school or college. Regrettably, through the centuries mankind has often punished people who have lived through their own innate or intuitive knowledge. It's easy enough to manipulate a crowd of people who rarely think for themselves, hence the burning of witches, and even herbalists who would have worked with the magical lore of plants, which arose from the Church's attempt to wipe out witchcraft in the UK and Europe during the 17th and 18th centuries. When people live in fear through ignorance they can easily accept someone else's word as the truth, rather than take responsibility for their own lives.

Introduction

So is magic against God? Or against the Bible? If you read the Bible you will be familiar with the quotation from the New Testament (in the gospels of Matthew and Luke): 'Ask, and it shall be given unto you; seek, and ye shall find. Knock, and the door shall be opened. For everyone who asks will receive, and everyone who seeks shall find, and the door will be opened to anyone who knocks.' Can it really be as simple as that? Do you really have to ask? Actually, yes, it is that simple!

If you find that statement difficult to believe, just think back on your own life and remember the times you have virtually asked for negative outcomes by saying or thinking, 'It'll never work out' / 'I'll never get a response' / 'I won't pass the exam', and so on. And what has been the outcome? If you are honest with yourself you will realize that you have talked yourself into problems rather than out of problems, just as I did. In Chapter 2 I explain some of my own story and how angel magic really did bring miracles into my life. That's why I want to share my experiences with you, and show you how easily you can bring angel magic into your life too.

About This Book

Magic is all about using the power of your word, thought and deed in tandem with the gifts of Mother Nature and the gifts of God. If you are looking for a book which gives 'evocations' (spells to bring a physical manifestation of an angel) then this book isn't for you. *The Book of Angel Magic* is based on the belief that your angel is here with you anyway, at all times. This book is more about 'invitations' than 'evocations'! I believe that it is very important to ask for an angel's help, and then be ready and willing to accept what is known as 'the perfect outcome', which is what the angels know is the right outcome for you and anyone else involved in your angelic quest.

In *The Book of Angel Magic* my intention is to introduce to you the joy of having your angels in your life, meeting them in a simple and easy way, and demystifying the belief that working with angels is somehow difficult or the ability of only a few special people. Angels are gifts from God for everyone. Each of us has the ability to communicate with them in whichever way is right for us, and each of us has the chance to bring their

magic into our lives in the simplest of ways. There is no need for expensive courses, testimonials, or initiation ceremonies, your angel is with you now, whether you know it or not, and the moment that you bring your angel into your life that is the moment when the magic will begin!

The Book of Angel Magic explains how to:

+ ***Create change magically*** – by releasing blocks and letting go of resistance. (Just bear in mind that the blocks or obstacles on our path are usually put there by ourselves, through our own fears)
+ ***Create love magically*** – by first forgiving and learning to love ourselves, then others
+ ***Create abundance magically*** – by opening to the never-ending good of Creation
+ ***Create a healthy environment*** for ourselves and the beings with whom we share our planet
+ ***Create a natural field of protection*** around ourselves, our families and our homes.

Rituals and Visualizations

Throughout this book you will find rituals and visualization exercises to help you connect with your angels and bring angelic magic into your life.

A visualization exercise is a way of relaxation in which you are encouraged to imagine yourself going on a journey in which you can enjoy certain experiences. The first step is to relax your entire body and your mind in order to let your creative side go on this journey. In a group situation, a leader will 'guide' others on this journey, or if you are alone you can pre-record the scripts given in this book and then play them back to yourself.

The word 'ritual' comes from the word 'rite' which is related to the Sanskrit word 'riti' meaning 'way' or 'custom'. By following certain customs you should find connecting with angelic magic both easy and enjoyable.

Before doing any of the visualization exercises in this book, find a place where you feel at peace, turn off the mobile, unplug the phone and put a big Do Not Disturb sign on the door

Introduction

if necessary. Then light at least one candle and ask the angels to be with you at this time. Apart from candlelight being calming and attractive, angels are 'beings of light', coming from the Light (God). I feel they can connect with you more easily when you are not bombarding your environment with electrical current.

The Universal Law of Ten-Fold Return

When performing angel magic, it is important not to manipulate anyone to act against their will, for to do this is to disempower them and you could never have a 'perfect outcome' if you did that. There is a law called 'The Universal Law of Ten-fold Return'. This promises that whatever you give out you get back ten times stronger! Just think of the figure 8, which is also like the symbol of infinity. Imagine you are standing at the bottom of the lower circle of the 8 and you send out a word such as 'Love'. The power of that word goes outwards, gains momentum as it reaches the opposite side of the figure 8, and rebounds back at you ten times stronger than when you first sent it outwards. (If you

---

have ever tried to keep up with the ball in a game of squash, you will know what I mean!) Anyone who works within this field is aware of this, so you can imagine what would happen in return if you give out a negative action or word! (In fact, as I mentioned earlier, when the Church burned witches and their cats in the 17th and 18th centuries, the UK and Europe was overrun by rats which brought plague and caused hundreds of thousands of deaths. That could be seen as their 'ten-fold return' coming back to them for their actions!) Certainly when working with angels, they will not help you do anything that is in any way manipulating the other person, or going against their natural will. Angel magic is pure and loving and can only bring good in return.

Angel magic is pure and loving and can only bring good in return.

What You Will Need

As I mentioned earlier, it costs very little to connect with angel magic. All you will need is a quiet place indoors or outside and, depending on the area you are working in:

+ **candles** (some rituals work more quickly with candles of a specific colour. If a colour is not mentioned in the following rituals, then trust your instincts and choose what colour you think best)
+ **angel figures** or **pictures**
+ **anything gold in colour** (to draw the golden energy of angels to you)
+ **incense sticks** (specific scents are mentioned in some of the rituals and you can also choose scents which you feel appropriate)
+ **card/paper**
+ **scissors** or **stanley knife**
+ **felt-tip pens, crayons** or **paints**

✦ **audio cassettes** and **recorder/player** if you wish to record
   the visualization exercises to play back to yourself

Some specific items are suggested in the rituals that follow.
However, if you can't afford them or if you can't find these
things close to hand, don't worry: the most important requirements for any of the rituals are loving thoughts and actions,
and those are freely available within you right now!

**The most important requirements for angel magic are
loving thoughts and actions.**

A Final Word

Are you ready to create change and bring love, abundance and
health into your life? It must begin with you, however, for the
only road to happiness and fulfilment is through yourself, not
through anyone else. That is really what the often overused
word 'empowerment' means. For instance, we cannot be happy
because we have made someone love us, we must learn to love
ourselves before we can attract love into our lives. Everything

we do acts as a magnet, so when we realize that we can create our own magic, then all sorts of magical things will come to us!

Everything we do acts as a magnet, so when we realize that we can create our own magic, then all sorts of magical things will come to us!

Chapter 1

All About Angels

Angels in History

As I mentioned in the Introduction, angels are considered to be 'messengers of God' who are sent by Him to undertake special missions with us humans here on Earth. Angels have been with us since pre-history, and their presence in our lives have been passed on for many centuries both orally, through stories and legends, and symbolically, through ceremonies and rituals.

From ancient records we know that supernatural, winged creatures were existing in the time of Mesopotamia and Sumeria. *Kabiru*, for instance, is where we get the word 'cherubum', and this is the Assyrian word for winged human forms which acted as 'guards' over Babylon and Sumeria. The Greeks and Romans, of course, had their own gods, protectors and *daimones*, which were spirits who came in both good and evil forms, the good ones being protectors. Hermes is the well-known winged 'messenger of the gods' to the Greeks, while in Roman terms he was Mercury. When Christianity came to these lands and the churches wanted to capture more 'flock' from the pagan believers, the daimones became what we now call 'demons' and were relegated to the lower echelons as something to be feared.

Four thousand years or so ago, in the more easterly lands of Persia and India, the people were connecting with *devas* (which means 'the shining ones'), who were closely related to the four elements of Earth, Fire, Air and Water, and the early texts of the Hindu (called the Veda) also mention these devas. These 'shining ones', messengers from the gods, were therefore introduced

firstly into Judaism and then Christianity as angels, and later into Islam, where they are known as *malaika*. So, angels, devas, kabiru, daimones and malaika are one and the same: shining messengers from God who collaborate with humans and the other beings on the planet in order to bring harmony and co-operation into our world.

One of the first written records of an angel appears in the Bible in the Book of Genesis, which according to various experts in biblical history place this at approximately 5,000 years BC. From this first mention in the Book of Genesis, to their last mention in the Book of Revelation, angels are recorded throughout both the Old and the New Testaments approximately 300 times.

In the Gospel of the Essenes (from the Lost Scrolls of the Essene Brotherhood), Jesus of Nazareth explains to his 'brotherhood' the importance of honouring the gifts of God, including the role of each of the angels and Mother Earth. In the Islamic faith, the prophet Mohammed was carried to heaven by angels and it was the archangel Gabriel who dictated to him what became the message of the Koran. Angels don't just look after

people for, according to Mohammed, 'Every raindrop that falls is accompanied by an Angel, for even a raindrop is a manifestation of being.' In more recent times, in 1820, Joseph Smith of Vermont, USA, met the angel Moroni while praying in a field, and this angel showed him where to find 'a book written on golden plates' which contained 'the fullness of the everlasting Gospel'. This became the basis of 'The Church of the Latter Day Saints', also known as the Mormons. These examples of angels being mentioned in the various religions proves again that angels come originally from God, and you do not have to follow a religion in order to connect with your own angels.

The Angelic Hierarchy

Over the centuries many scholars have developed theses about the hierarchy of angels. It seems that mankind needs to categorize angels in this way, just as we tend to have hierarchies in our political, educational and religious systems. It was during the 7th century AD that Pope Gregory the Great proclaimed there are nine 'orders of angels': angels, archangels, principalities,

powers, virtues, dominions, thrones, cherubim and seraphim. The archangels, guardian angels and princes (principalities) are apparently the angels which connect directly with people and look after our planet. But do angels really form in a hierarchical manner? I try not to get caught up in such questions, instead trust that the right angel will be with me when I am in need.

Angelic Names

Do angels have names? Perhaps it is just our human need which requires angels to be given names in order for us to communicate more easily with them. Hebrew records of angels tell us some of their names. (Note the suffix ' –el' or '–il' is Hebrew for 'of the Lord', so you will notice that all angel names end in this.) While Michael is named as the 'chief of princes' in the Book of Daniel, we know him as one of the four major archangels. The other three major archangels are Gabriel, Raphael and Uriel: Gabriel is said to rule the seraphim, while Raphael has the 'healing hand of the divine', and Uriel is the archangel for the physical world and the planet Earth.

Lists of names of angels and archangels differ depending on what source you are researching, from Christian to Talmudic, to the Kabbalists. The Koran, for instance, also names four archangels: Jibraiil (also known as Gabriel), Mika'il (Michael), Azrael (Raphael, here known as the Angel of Death) and Israfel (the angel who plays the last trumpet at the end of the day and who shall wake the dead on the Day of Judgement). Again, depending on what source you read, the archangels were created at different times, but Michael, Uriel, Gabriel and Raphael (also known as Ramiel) are usually named together. The main thing is not to get dogmatic about angels' names. The priority is to get in touch with them, whatever their name!

The Four Archangels

Archangels are mentioned in many Christian, Islamic and Jewish holy books, especially the Bible and the Koran. They also play a major role in the Kabbalah (a Jewish esoteric doctrine) where one is assigned to each divine emanation. I see the archangels as the 'overseers' of the planet and all that

happens here, while guardian angels are 'supervisors' who are in charge of giving us humans direction! If it was a business organization, I would imagine God as being the chairman, the archangels being management, and the guardian angels being the workers! Humans would take on the role of 'clients'!

Because the archangels relate to so many belief systems, here is some interesting information concerning each one:

ARCHANGEL GABRIEL

Known as 'man of God' or 'God is my strength', he is the one angel who is mentioned several times in the Bible bringing messages to people as, for example, in the Book of Daniel (8:16–27) when he gave messages of hope to Daniel, and in the Gospel of Luke (1:11–22) when he announced the birth of John the Baptist, and then later in Luke (1:26–38) when he announced the birth of Jesus. Gabriel appeared to both the Virgin Mary and also to the prophet Mohammed, so he was given some very important messages to convey to us humans, no matter what our race or creed. Gabriel is also the archangel of creativity and the arts.

Direction:	Gabriel is the Angel of the West.
Element:	Water.
Zodiac Signs:	Cancer, Scorpio and Pisces.
Tasks:	To bring hope, justice, creativity and intuition to the greater consciousness of mankind.
Day/s:	Monday.
Planet:	The Moon.
Colours:	Silver, white and blue.

ARCHANGEL URIEL

Uriel (known as 'fire of God') could been seen nowadays as the 'ecological angel' who looks after the planet Earth and all who inhabit it. In the Kabbalah he is noted as being assigned to the 'middle pillar of the Tree of Life'. In the Chronicles of Enoch, the prophet Enoch describes Uriel as 'one of the holy angels who is over the world, the leader of them all', and Enoch records, 'Uriel showed to me the Sun, Moon and Stars, all the ministering creatures which make their revolution in the chariots of the heavens.'

Uriel's feast day is July 28, the time between the harvest of the hay and the harvest of the corn.

Direction:	Uriel is the Angel of the East.
Element:	Air.
Zodiac Signs:	Gemini, Libra and Aquarius.
Tasks:	To ensure constant, cyclical change in our planet and our lives. To bring about universal cosmic consciousness.
Day/s:	Tuesday and Friday.
Planet:	Uranus
Colours:	Violet, white and indigo.

ARCHANGEL MICHAEL

Michael is also known as 'Who is as God'. He is here to defend the weak and protect those who are facing dangers of any sort. Pictorially he is shown as slaying a dragon, which can be symbolic of a protector who helps us overpower our fears.

Direction:	Michael is the Angel of the North.
Element:	Earth.
Zodiac Signs:	Taurus, Virgo and Capricorn.
Tasks:	To protect those who face difficulties along their pathway of life. Michael can bring us patience, motivation, ambition and protection as we move forward to personal empowerment.
Day/s:	Thursday and Sunday.
Planet:	Mercury.
Colours:	Orange, white and gold.

Archangel Raphael

Raphael (or Ramiel) means 'God has healed'. Raphael rules the seraphim (the angels gifted with love and light) and one of his duties is to oversee the evening winds. He is the archangel in charge of the physical body, of healing, health and longevity.

Direction:	Raphael is the Angel of the South.
Element:	Fire.
Zodiac Signs:	Aries, Leo and Sagittarius.
Tasks:	To bring love, joy, light and knowledge into our lives, and is particularly charged with the current universal interest in angelic healing throughout the world.
Planet:	Mercury.
Day/s:	Wednesday and Saturday.
Colours:	Yellow, white and grey.

Working with the Archangels

If you wish to bring some extra healing into a particular area of your life, ask for help from the archangel in charge (as shown above). It also helps to bring their angelic magic into your life by doing the chosen rituals, as described later in this book, on the day relating to that particular archangel, and remembering which one looks after your specific zodiac sign (see overleaf).

ANGELS FOR EACH DAY OF THE WEEK

When you wish to attract the particular strengths of these archangels into your life, it will happen more effectively if you call on them on their specific day of the week, and have something in their colour to honour them. For instance, if you are asking for help from archangel Gabriel, you might like to use a silver candlestick with a blue candle and/or wear something in these colours.

DAY	ANGEL	COLOUR
Monday	Gabriel	silver, white, blue
Tuesday	Uriel	violet, white, indigo
Wednesday	Raphael	yellow, white, grey
Thursday	Michael	orange, white, gold
Friday	Uriel	violet, white, indigo
Saturday	Raphael	yellow, white, grey
Sunday	Michael	orange, white, gold

All About Angels

ANGELS FOR EACH ZODIAC SIGN

ZODIAC SIGN	ARCHANGEL	ELEMENT
Aries *(March 21–April 20)*	Raphael	Fire
Taurus *(April 21–May 20)*	Michael	Earth
Gemini *(May 21–June 20)*	Uriel	Air
Cancer *(June 21–July 22)*	Gabriel	Water
Leo *(July 23–August 22)*	Raphael	Fire
Virgo *(August 23–September 22)*	Michael	Earth

Angel Magic

Libra	Uriel	Air
(September 23–October 22)		

Scorpio	Gabriel	Water
(October 23–November 21)		

Sagittarius	Raphael	Fire
(November 22–December 21)		

Capricorn	Michael	Earth
(December 22–January 20)		

Aquarius	Uriel	Air
(January 21–February 18)		

Pisces	Gabriel	Water
(February 19 –March 20)		

Yes, there is an archangel for the four elements of the astrological zodiac. Check out which one looks after your birth chart

(see above) and be aware that you can call on this archangel's help in time of need throughout the year. The four elements are Fire, Earth, Air and Water – here is a brief look at the main characteristics of each element, and how the archangels can help:

Fire Element: Fire people may express themselves with great passion and enthusiasm, but their flame may quickly quench itself when they feel low. Surround yourself with candlelight when you feel this way and ask Raphael to re-ignite your inner passion to help see you through any dark times.

Earth Element: Earth people are usually practical, hard working, reliable and dutiful, but sometimes they may get stuck in a rut and find it difficult to get free. Ask Michael to help you lift your head up so that you can see a different route to follow and protect you from your fear of change.

Air Element: Usually open-minded and quick-thinkers, who want to share their knowledge and ideas with others, Air

people may become dogmatic and rigid in their beliefs. Uriel can help you clear your head and lighten up your thought patterns should they become clogged with outmoded ideas!

Water Element: The most sensitive of all the elements, Water people are usually very intuitive and spiritual. Because they are also the most sensitive of the signs, they can become withdrawn and fearful. Gabriel can fill your heart with the love you need to share your sensitivity and intuition with others.

Angels of the Calendar Year

When my sisters and I were children we would vie with each other to be the first to say 'White Rabbits!' on the morning of the first day of a new month and so bring good fortune into our lives. There is a simpler way to ensure that you are doing the right thing at the right time, and that is to connect with the angels of the calendar year. According to some sources an angel is assigned to each month of the calendar, and when we

connect with it we can be helped in special ways as we go through the pastoral year. By welcoming in the angel of each new month, we become more mindful of the changes we need to face each month and each year of our lives. We also become more aware of the opportunities of working with the natural energy of the seasons. As the new month begins, simply light a candle and greet the angel of the month by name. Ask it to help you be mindful of the changes taking place in your life and to help you face any challenges on your path. Check out which angel can help you right now, and recognize what you might need to do at this time.

Note: The following is written for the Northern Hemisphere. For readers in the Southern Hemisphere, where the seasons are experienced differently, I have included the alternative month in brackets.

THE ANGEL OF JANUARY – GABRIEL

*(Southern Hemisphere – Gabriel is the Angel of **July**)*

A time for inner knowledge, for contemplating how far we have come and to where we are heading. A healthy introspection is

one gift we can receive from the angel Gabriel who comes to us as a wise spirit helping us find warmth in the cold of winter.

THE ANGEL OF FEBRUARY - BARCHIEL

*(Southern Hemisphere – Barchiel is the Angel of **August**)*

This month is often known as 'fill the ditch' time because of its rain and snow. During this time we may have to face some elemental obstacles and, though we know that Spring is on the horizon, we can lose faith easily. The angel Barchiel brings us light in the darkness and the gift of patience as we await a new dawning of growth.

THE ANGEL OF MARCH - MACHIDIEL

*(Southern Hemisphere – Machidiel is the Angel of **September**)*

Spring is coming at last! With the help of the angel Machidiel we can enjoy a boost to our inner strength and courage which will help us begin to sow the seeds that later we shall be harvesting. It is with this angel that we celebrate the Spring Equinox, the symbol of balance between the Sun and Moon (fire of action and receptivity of intuition).

All About Angels

THE ANGEL OF APRIL - ASMODEL

*(Southern Hemisphere – Asmodel is the Angel of **October**)*

This month is the time of renewal and rebirth. Now that the Sun is shining and the days are longer we have the energy to try new things, meet new people, look to new horizons.

All around us we can celebrate the gift of new life with the angel Asmodel.

THE ANGEL OF MAY - AMBIEL

*(Southern Hemisphere – Ambiel is the Angel of **November**)*

At one of the most abundant times of the year, the angel Ambiel helps us to bring alive that deep-seated creative spark within each of us. Now is the time to thank the devic kingdom for their constant support and wonderful gifts of nature. (The devas are angels who look after nature.)

THE ANGEL OF JUNE - MURIEL

*(Southern Hemisphere – Muriel is the Angel of **December**)*

Now we really see nature at her best as we are offered the peace and stability of knowing that our harvest is guaranteed

later on. We may need to pluck some weeds from our abundant growth, but the angel Muriel can help us enjoy such a task in the company of loving and supportive friends and family under the light of the Summer Solstice.

THE ANGEL OF JULY - VERCHIEL

*(Southern Hemisphere – Verchiel is the Angel of **January**)*

The angel Verchiel will help us to enjoy and appreciate the benefits of the sometimes backbreaking work we have put into our lives. Often we are so busy working and pushing ourselves forward that we forget to stop and simply stare. This angel will remind us that there is a time for work and a time for relaxation.

THE ANGEL OF AUGUST - HAMALIEL

*(Southern Hemisphere – Hamaliel is the Angel of **February**)*

Often we take for granted some of the gifts we have been given. In order to make the most of what we have, we must not turn away from the need to tend carefully what we have begun. The angel Hamaliel will help us maintain our stamina when we need to put extra effort into our lives.

All About Angels

THE ANGEL OF SEPTEMBER - URIEL

*(Southern Hemisphere – Uriel is the Angel of **March**)*

It's almost time to harvest what we have planted, tended and enjoyed. Some of the things we worked on may begin to die away now, and we may be reluctant to let things go. The angel Uriel will help us see that there is a valid reason for each season and even when things come to a natural end they can still give us nourishment.

THE ANGEL OF OCTOBER - BARBIEL

*(Southern Hemisphere – Barbiel is the Angel of **April**)*

It's harvest time at last! Now look back over the months and see just how far you have come! The angel Barbiel reminds us of the generosity of nature and at this time helps us understand 'as you reap, so shall you sow'. Some things we shall enjoy immediately, others we can keep until the optimum time.

Angel Magic

THE ANGEL OF NOVEMBER - ADNACHIEL

*(Southern Hemisphere – Adnachiel is the Angel of **May**)*

If you have worked hard you will be thankful for the benefits of the harvest which will now support you through the coming winter. As the days grow shorter, the angel Adnachiel urges us to show thanks to others who have supported us throughout the year, not least the beings of the devic kingdom.

THE ANGEL OF DECEMBER - HANAEL

*(Southern Hemisphere – Hanael is the Angel of **June**)*

The nights are long, the hours of the Sun short. It is time to remember to look after the angels of the natural kingdom, the devas, and ensure they are safe and comfortable from the ravages of winter. Bring some greenery into your house and invite the devas to dwell in your home during the cold, frosty season. The angel Hanael will help us enjoy the balance of giving and receiving.

Chapter 2
Angel Experiences

'Within each of our spirits there is our Self and many angels,' I was recently told by one of my angels. I believe that we have each been given an angel to look after us from the moment our spirit decides to take the journey to Earth in order to learn certain lessons on the pathway to spiritual and personal development.

There are many references to angels in the works of some of the world's greatest writers over the centuries. Apart from the epic works of John Milton, Dante Alighieri and John Donne, angels were also brought into William Shakespeare's

plays including *Hamlet* and *Romeo and Juliet*, while Mark Twain, William Blake, Paulo Coelho, Byron, John Ruskin, Robert Browning, George Bernard Shaw, Leo Tolstoy and G. K. Chesterton, to name just a few, all made some mention of them in their work. The Catholic priest Padre Pio wrote about the help he received from his angels, as did many papal leaders such as Pope John XXIII and Pope Paul VI, but somehow the general public seems to have lost contact. It seems that it is only when we become entrenched in the age of empirical science that we tend to lose sight of them. As Pope John Paul I said in 1978: 'Angels are the great strangers in this time. It is necessary to speak much more about them as ministers of providence in the government of the world and men.'

High-Profile Believers

While some people may dismiss the recent upsurge in interest in angels as merely 'para-religion' or 'New Age nonsense', there are many high-profile believers who have openly spoken of their knowledge of these heavenly beings in their lives. They were certainly courageous to do so, as up to recently it really wasn't the thing to do! One immediately risked the possibility of being labelled 'eccentric' at best and 'plain crazy' at worst, but still they persisted in sharing their experiences. People often ask me why there has been such a change in attitude in recent years. There's been a lot of talk about The Age of Aquarius dawning and so bringing with it a seismic shift in consciousness. Though Aquarius is an Air sign, it also symbolizes the Water Bearer, someone who brings a constant flow of knowledge onto the Earth. We have also moved from the 1900s to the 2,000s and, according to the science of numbers, this is a giant step from feeling abandoned, lost and isolated to realizing we have choices, and perhaps co-operation with others may be the key to fulfilment. Whatever the reason for the change, it's as though the realms between heaven and earth are becoming closer, as though the angels are reaching down and touching us gently, encouraging us to speak out.

Angel Magic

BILLY GRAHAM, EVANGELIST

The American Evangelist Billy Graham has often spoken of angels since he began his preaching almost half a century ago. In an interview in *Midwest Today* [December 1992] he is quoted as saying: 'Angels belong to a uniquely different dimension of creation we can scarcely comprehend. He has given angels higher knowledge, power and mobility than we. They are God's messengers ... ministering spirits, whose chief business is to carry out His orders in the world. He has given them an ambassadorial charge. He has designated and empowered them as holy deputies. Angels speak. They appear and reappear. They are emotional creatures ...'

DR JOHN C. LILLY, SCIENTIST

The American scientist Dr John C. Lilly, who worked with the US Air Force and the Department of Health, and is probably known better for his observations on dolphins' systems of communication, is not afraid to speak openly of his belief in angels. His autobiography, *The Scientist*, explains how he met his guardian angel in his childhood and how they communicated together from that time.

PADRE PIO

In 1887 a young boy was born to a farming family in Pietrelcina, Italy. He later became a monk with the stigmata etched in his hands, feet and side and was known as Padre Pio. This monk never failed to speak to and of his angel who, he said, he had met in his early years. The two were close friends and he often learned of other people's needs through his angel, rather than through the telecommunications of that day! In this way he sent healing to others even though the person may live on the other side of the world. Other people heard and saw his angels, too. Once his fellow monks heard voices singing in heavenly harmony and couldn't find the source. Padre Pio explained they were the angels bringing souls to heaven. When he died on September 22 1968, some tourists from the USA, who were in Italy at the time, saw angels in the sky that night, and they say they disappeared as the Sun rose in the morning.

PIERRE JOVANOVIC, JOURNALIST

The French journalist Pierre Jovanovic set out specifically to investigate these beings because of some unexpected happenings

in his own life. He set about his book with a journalist's require-
ment to find proof before publishing, and the answers are in *An
Enquiry into the Existence of Guardian Angels*, which has been
translated into English. Jovanovic began his search after he realized he had been saved by angelic intervention when he was shot
at by a sniper. He began with an open but healthily sceptical
mind. Many 'coincidences' got him in touch with his angels. 'The
first time, you tell yourself it was only an accident. The second
time, when someone gives you a book about the theme of Angels
in art, you think it's a real coincidence. The third time, you
receive a letter that begins "You are my guardian Angel ..." you
tell yourself it's an incredible simultaneity. The fourth time
leaves you speechless. After the tenth time, you surrender, and
after the twentieth you start talking seriously to your Angel.'

HEALTH PROFESSIONALS

Those who have worked with the dying, such as Dr Elizabeth
Kubler-Ross, Dr Raymond Moody, Professor Kenneth Ring and
Dr Melvin Morse, have all researched fascinating experiences of
angelic meetings in 'near-death experiences', some of which are

discussed later in this chapter. Francoise Dolto, the child psychoanalyst, is also open about her closeness to angels, and she openly asks for their daily protection.

WELLKNOWN WRITERS

In her autobiographical book, *The Eagle and the Rose*, English-woman Rosemary Altea records a personal spiritual experience which also involved angels. She prayed daily, asking for God's help, and once she asked for a sign to know she was doing the right thing developing as a medium and so acting as a go-between for the bereaved and those in spirit. She relates how she got an immediate response: 'I knew instinctively who they were. I heard them quite distinctly and in total harmony. I heard them singing, angels – singing! Clear and sweet.'

In the mid-1950s there was a little five-year-old girl in the USA who was terrified of everything, and especially of going to sleep, just in case she never woke up again. One night an angel appeared to her and told her, 'Always remember, there is nothing to be afraid of.' That little girl is Eileen Elias Freeman, who has since written several books on angels including *Touched by Angels* and *Angelic Healing*.

What Do Angels Look Like?

'Tis only when they spring to heaven that angels reveal themselves to you,' said Robert Browning, but that may not be so. Generally speaking, as angels are 'beings of light' they are seen as light. Often one may feel the surrounding energy change as the connection is first made: it may get hot or it may get cold. Most people who have seen angels describe them as 'bright', 'a shining light', 'like humans, except it was as though a light bulb shone inside its body.' Others see 'flashes of light like the trails a firework leaves behind it.' (They are 'beings of light' and therefore travel at the speed of light!) I find it easiest to see them when there is little or no interference from radio/televisual energies or even electric light bulbs! I usually watch TV by candlelight for this reason.

Mostly I have seen angels as either little balls of bright energy which dance around the room, or as larger-than-life outlines of human form made of very bright golden light. If you are desperate to see them in order to prove to yourself that they exist, try not to stare at any 'vision' that you see.

Instead, look with what is known as your 'third eye', which is really your spiritual centre, based in the small dip between your eyebrows. So that means that if you think you saw an angel about, rather than stare unblinking at it, look instead just a little to the left or right of where the image presented itself. It is really what is known as looking 'out of the corner of your eye' and it can require some practice.

Emma Heathcote, an eminent theologist based at the University of Birmingham, has studied several hundred people's experiences of 'meeting' with angels. A quarter said they saw their angel with wings, a fifth met their angel in human form, who appeared suddenly and, just as suddenly, disappeared. The remainder felt a presence, smelled an unusual perfume, saw a figure in white or felt enveloped in an angel's wings. While it is generally accepted that young children are very psychic and find such meetings quite an everyday occurrence, the interesting thing from Ms Heathcote's studies is that most of these people were aged between 36 and 55 years.

Angels can also look just like ordinary people, especially when they seem to suddenly appear out of 'nowhere' to help out in times of crisis. One element people agree on in these instances is that their eyes are 'arresting' and the words they speak are never forgotten.

Angels to the Rescue!

While the cynic may dismiss the idea of seeing angels as being just fanciful, there was one spectacular sighting of an angel during the First World War which was seen by many people and had an immediate effect on the spectators.

During the Great War (1914–1918), as it became known, thousands of soldiers on either side lost their lives trying to gain a metre or two of land against 'the enemy', especially near the border between France and Belgium. The battles fought in the trenches were the most horrific, where men in both camps were ordered to certain death by their superior officers as they left the relative safety of their trench and went 'over the line'. One place which shall remain in the minds of many is Mons in

Belgium. There it seemed that the Allies were certainly going to lose the battle and their lives, as they were what remained of only two regiments and they were hopelessly outnumbered by the Germans.

Just when all seemed lost, a bright being 'with yellow hair and golden armour and riding on a white horse' came to their aid, 'looking for all the world like Saint George, the patron saint of England', said the British soldiers. To the Germans, under the command of General von Kluck, it appeared that archangel Michael had come to the rescue of their enemies, as his light shone on what looked like thousands of British troops lying in position against them. Their horses refused to move forward at the sight, they turned sharply and fled the field of battle. This story has been related by many soldiers on both the Allied and the German sides. It was a turning point in the Battle of Mons and gave great hope and security to those embattled British soldiers. So startling was the event that many spoke about it afterwards, despite the fear of possible ridicule. Now that's what I call angel magic!

More than two decades later during the Second World War, in the small village of Budaliget near Budapest, Hungary, four

young people met together in an underground shelter to seek spiritual help as they faced the cataclysmic events of Hitler's army marching into their country. It was 1943, and one of the three women there, Gitta Mallasz, suddenly began to channel messages from an angel. These messages helped them survive the bloodshed of the Second World War, and after the war Gitta followed the career of a graphic artist. It was not until the early 1960s that she began to spread the word of what had happened, and these experiences then became a book entitled *Talking with Angels*.

Angels and Near-Death Experiences

In more recent years an American doctor, Raymond Moody, began one of the first studies on what are now termed 'near-death experiences' (NDE). This is where the person's spirit leaves their physical body due to grave illness or trauma, and for whatever reason then returns to the body which comes back to life once more.

During these near-death experiences many people, young and old, have had wonderful spiritual visions. Firstly, they tend to leave their body and see it beneath them as they lift free of their physical presence. Then what they term 'a Light' or 'a Light Being' comes to them and leads them on a journey during which time they often go back through earlier experiences and review what occurred. At some point they are given the chance to return to their body or to stay in 'heaven'. These experiences are always recorded as being life changing, giving the person more insight into their own purpose in life. Many of those who have undergone an NDE have seen angels and felt healed by their meeting.

In his book, *Parting Visions*, Dr Melvin Morse says that in his own research at least 50% of children in his studies see guardian angels as a part of their near-death experiences and later these angels may reappear in order to help in times of crisis.

In earlier times the medical profession tended to dismiss such experiences as 'hallucinations', yet way back in the late 1920s Sir William Barrett, a physics professor at the Royal College of Science in Dublin, Ireland, undertook a systematic

study of 'deathbed visions'. His was the first scientific study to conclude that the mind of a dying patient is often clear and rational. In more recent years, Wilder Penfield, the father of modern neuro-science, has documented the fact that we have an area in the right temporal lobe of the brain which he calls the 'circuit boards of mysticism'.

But what about the possibility of seeing what we expect to see, through earlier indoctrination in religion and culture? It certainly is possible, but is it probable? Taking information from Dr Melvin Morse's book mentioned above, why did only 50% of the children observed see angels? More than likely closer to 100% would have been told something about angels if they had been brought up in a religion, be it Jewish, Christian, Muslim, and so forth. Also, there are instances of children who never knew about angels yet saw them when they went through their NDE. Dr Morse records that several of the children studied were disappointed to see angels with no wings. One child sat up in bed and said, 'Angels, I see angels!' Then the girl looked puzzled and demanded, 'Why aren't they wearing any wings?' As Dr Morse asks: 'If deathbed visions were simply a fantasy of

the mind, why would this little girl have seen something differ-ent from her expectations?' Why, indeed!

Americans aren't the only race that records near-death expe-riences. In Australia, Dr Cherie Sutherland, a visiting research fellow in the school of sociology at the University of New South Wales, has also studied near-death experiences. She has pub-lished her findings in her books *Transformed by the Light*, *Children of the Light* and *In the Company of Angels*. In one instance, a little girl named Penelope was in a coma for five days. When she came back to consciousness, she related 'I've been to the angels. I wasn't scared. When I was with the angels there was a mummy angel and a daddy angel with a big white beard, and lots of angels coming and going. When I asked to come home the grandpa angel brought me back.' Another girl, Helen, who had travelled through the tunnel into the bright light says, 'I heard this music but I don't know where it was coming from, and I can't even describe what it sounded like. I was thinking "I didn't know there were so many notes between the notes we know."' Another subject, Hannah, was also amazed at what she heard. 'Then I heard music,' she says.

'I can't describe it in earthly terms. I still hear it sometimes. It's like panpipes but beyond anything here.'

My Own Story

From early childhood I always knew about angels. It may have begun when I was only a few months old and became very ill, necessitating a long time away from my parents while I visited hospital after hospital as they tried to find out what ailed me. I vaguely remember feeling cut off from the nurses who would peek into my cot every now and again and greet me. It seemed that I had my own little world within my cot and didn't need them! Then I got better and returned home, but I was always pretty quiet and didn't even speak a recognizable language till I was four years old! Like most children, I was brought up with pictures of a guardian angel who would be looking after me always, and when I said my prayers at night I would include a prayer to this being. This was nothing special in my peer group – we all knew about angels and we all prayed to them. So what happened then? Why did most people discard them as they

grew up? I can only presume that as we learn the 'three R's' and develop our rational left brain more than our intuitive right brain, we tend to cut away from that world which cannot be proven and is rarely seen. And, of course, if the subject comes up we fear ridicule if we speak out!

For some reason, though, I didn't let go of my angel, I always knew it was around. I presumed everyone else knew they had one too, and was quite shocked to discover in my mid-20s that I seemed to be in a minority of one in this belief! The discovery made me feel extremely immature and very foolish and at that moment I walked away from my angel and stopped listening. Fortunately for me, my angel was still beside me though I completely ignored this for many years. It wasn't until I was going through a very rough patch about ten years later that I opened up my eyes and ears again and began to once more communicate with my angel. This time, though, I kept it quiet!

I believe that I am a walking example of how angels can help you transform your life into something magical. Back in the early 90s I was miserable, depressed, unemployed and pretty much penniless. Despite the fact that I am neither lazy nor

incapable of learning new skills, every time I got a job something would go wrong and I would find myself unemployed again. Yet I still had a mortgage to pay and all the other everyday expenses of living. My life was a nightmare, and nightmares also came to me in my dreams! I was desperately seeking a way out of this fearful state, and I kept asking the angels for help. During this time I would get messages from them, but I was so low in self-esteem that I couldn't understand what they meant. Still, I wrote them down and they now make sense to me. (You can read more about these messages in Chapter 3).

On June 29, 1994, I was lying under a tree in my garden, wondering what to do, when I was given an angelic message which said 'Give a course called "Talking with Angels"'. It came to me in a voice that I had learned to believe over the years: kind and comforting, yet insistent and definite. I had asked for help and I was given it! I followed the message and so I began giving workshops and courses of the same title all around Ireland. At that time, however, I was afraid people would consider me crazy, but I gave the courses anyway and fortunately

got a lot of positive media attention – and made a huge circle of worthwhile friends and colleagues – which has continued to this day.

In the intervening years I have taken my angel courses to many places, including France, Australia and the UK. I have also written a book called *Open Your Heart to Angel Love*, created meditative tapes and produced my own 'Angel Inspiration Cards' using the messages I have received from my angels over the years. (See Chapter 3 on how to make your own Inspiration Cards.) Of course, this did not all happen overnight, but once you believe angelic help can bring magic into your life you can put the first steps toward fulfilling your own wishes into action. I did. I often relate this as 'Fear knocked on my door. My angel helped me open it. There was nothing there.' Fear is the biggest block we all have to face. With angel magic we can discover it doesn't even exist!

Only a few short years ago I asked my angel to help me find a career where I could mainly work from home, didn't have to get involved with traffic gridlock, and could get a good income from it. Almost immediately magic happened. The phone rang

and I was asked to write a regular column for a magazine, which in turn developed into a weekly column for a newspaper, and within a year I was also given a weekly radio spot on a national radio station. To make the change even more miraculous, I was given another weekly spot on a national television programme! What a remarkable turnaround, and all due to my angel's help! For several years I would ask the angels to manifest certain things in my life: money, a new car, and so on. Now I have been given one of the best gifts of all: peace of mind. It doesn't mean things don't 'go wrong' in my life, it just means that if something doesn't turn out like I would have wished it, I understand there is a reason for it. That reason usually proves itself to be because there is something better with my name on it! You could call it angel magic – I do.

Over the years I have had regular 'angelic experiences'. These experiences are not necessarily of the 'Road to Damascus' variety, but they have had some long-term positive effects on my life, which I will explain later. Often we may think that we need to have bolts of lightning flashing across the sky and

rumbles of thunder from the heavens in order to know that the angels are close by, but it is quite the opposite in my case.

Take this example. I had begun my angel workshops in October 1994 and, when I was out walking in the nearby park during that Autumn, I collected three fallen Japanese maple leaves which I then carried in my hardback notebook for my workshops. I knew by then that I had three angels watching over me and these leaves would remind me of their presence when I was talking to groups. Over the months as I travelled around Ireland with my work, the three leaves carried in my notebook dried and crumbled and I thought no more about them. The following June a stroke of good fortune (no doubt as a gift from the angels!) gave me the chance to travel to Australia for free so naturally I grabbed the offer and arrived in Sydney on June 20, the eve of the Winter Solstice downunder. The next day I was in a large indoor shopping mall, feeling very lost and confused, no doubt due to jetlag. I was convinced that I had somehow left my angels behind me in Ireland, or en route to the Antipodes, and that perhaps I would never be able to get back to them again! As I walked around this glass-enclosed

marketplace I worried and worried about this loss. Suddenly I noticed on the pavement in front of me a Japanese maple leaf, a deep red/orange autumnal colour, just like the ones I had been carrying with me in previous workshops. I stopped and picked it up, then looked around me and nowhere was there any type of deciduous tree, and as it was wintertime in Sydney there would certainly be no leaves left at this time. I just knew it was a message from the angels saying 'Don't worry, we're here with you on your present path.' Feeling half foolish and half delighted, I carried the maple leaf back with me to Ireland on my return journey and put it into my workshop notebook. Despite the fact that I have brought that notebook with me to every workshop I give, both at home and abroad, over the intervening years, that Japanese maple leaf is in the same pristine condition in which I found it back in 1995! Another piece of angel magic.

The angels seem to like working with Mother Nature because in another instance, this time during an Irish winter, I was feeling depressed and useless and I went for a walk in the nearby Phoenix Park. There is a section in the park, which is called the

'People's Garden', where there are ornamental trees and shrubs. However, as this was January there were few, if any, flowers or, indeed, people to be seen! Just as I walked through the gates leading to the pond I found a bunch of lilacs, which looked as though they had been hastily picked from a bush, lying up against the gate. I had to pass them in order to enter, so I did. But something told me to go back and pick them up. Sure enough they were freshly cut lilac blossoms (which happen to be one of my favourite flowers) and they are, of course, purple in colour, the symbol of spiritual energy. After looking around for some time and finding no one about I accepted them as a gift and brought them home with me. More 'angel magic'!

Sometimes angels can give you a beautiful scent just to let you know that they are with you. In my case it is usually one of flowers, and just to show it is from my angels they are out of season, such as hyacinths in Autumn or roses in December. One evening I was driving home from a workshop in Galway, on the west coast of Ireland. It is a long drive and a tiring one, especially after a full day's workshop. I had a companion in the car with me and I was just wondering if I should continue

driving when the entire car filled up with a powerful pine essence. My companion also noticed it. That essence enlivened me and helped me to drive home without feeling tired any more. Do be alert to these small but definite magical messages because they can happen to you too!

Often when we are too busy to listen during our waking hours, our angels will come to us in our dreams. I have had many helpful dreams which have moved me from feelings of despair and poverty-consciousness to a reality of joy and abundance.

Often when we are too busy to listen during our waking hours, our angels will come to us in our dreams.

I had a particularly vivid dream in February 1993, which I have never forgotten. At the time things were not going well for me and I had just taken on a job writing freelance copy for a magazine. I had no car and there seemed little chance of ever affording one again. Then I had this dream. It was brief but vivid. In it my angel was standing to my right and we were at the back of a red hatchback car. My angel was insisting 'This is for you' and pointing in particular to the small lip at the top of

the back window. When I awoke I remembered the dream and knew without a doubt that I would soon own a red hatchback car with a lip at the top of the back window. I hadn't a clue what make it would be, so I spent the next few days searching car parks to find this idiosyncrasy. At last I discovered it was a Peugeot 205. Within the month I had been made editor of the magazine and my income had increased. In this short time I had gone from believing I would never again own a car to searching the newspaper columns for the right one! Then I saw it advertised: Peugeot 205 Hatchback ... It was a reasonably recent model and an affordable price. I rang up the garage and asked the colour. 'Red' the salesman affirmed, and I arranged to take it on a test drive the following day. (He must have thought 'Typical woman, choosing a car by its colour!') I bought the car and kept it for more than five years, and it took me all over the country with rarely a complaint! I called it my 'dream machine' because it was such a wonderful trouble-free motorcar and, of course, I was given it in my dreams.

Eventually the time came to change the car and I toured Dublin looking for an up-to-date model of a Peugeot 205. Each

time I found one it seemed to slip from my grasp; there would be some reason why I couldn't buy it. Finally I said, 'Angels, can you please help me find the perfect car!' I then had a dream I was driving a car, and I didn't know what it was, only that it had a different interior to the one I was used to. My angel's voice said, 'Go to the garage on the North Circular Road.' Now at the time I lived on that very same road but for some reason had completely missed the fact that there was a car salesroom about a kilometre down the road from me! So I went there that day and a particular car seemed to stand out, almost as though it had flashed its headlights at me. Instead of test driving their Peugeot I asked to try the one which had caught my eye. It was an automatic Nissan Almera, much more opulent than anything I had driven before, yet the moment I sat in it I knew it was for me. And so it proved to be. See how quickly the angels can sort things out for you? But you must first ask, and then listen!

Another angelic dream which changed my life was given to me when I had first begun my 'Talking With Angels' workshops. I was still rather shaky in both my finances and my self-esteem, and things seemed to be going rather slowly. One night in

October 1994 I had a vivid and memorable dream in which I was handed a huge bouquet of flowers and the next thing I saw was a daffodil right in front of my face. Again, there was no 'Road to Damascus', it was as simple and short as that. I knew when I awoke that I was being promised good reason for celebration and congratulation (the symbol of being handed a bouquet of flowers), and that it would come in the Spring (when the daffodils were out). This kept me going through a bleak winter during which I was constantly asking my angels for help and confirmation that I was doing the right thing. Then the following February a journalist came to one of my workshops, asked if she could write an article about me, and the coverage came out in April 1995. The response was phenomenal! It was not until some time later I looked again at my photograph in the magazine. I was sitting at my kitchen table and on it was ... a vase full of daffodils! These dreams were short, to the point, vivid in colour and totally memorable. A sure sign they were from my angels.

My last two house purchases, which have proven to be most successful, have both been instigated by my angels. One

morning back in January 1990 I woke up and decided I wanted to sell my house south of the river in Dublin. Being single and having no children, I am in a position where I have no one else to consider when it comes to such a decision. I didn't know where I wanted to move to, only that I definitely wanted to sell up! I spent weeks searching and even put a deposit down on a house about a mile away, but that didn't work out. One day, after asking my angels to help me find my new home, I got into my car and drove across the river and found myself parking in a small village district on the north side. (I knew very little about the north side simply because I had always lived and worked south of the river and my friends lived there, too.) Not knowing quite why I had landed at this spot, I got out of the car and discovered the parking space was outside an estate agent's office. Looking in the window I saw a house which immediately attracted my attention. I ran into the office and discovered the representative was at that moment showing the house to prospective purchasers. Well ... I bought it! It was a wise move and it introduced me to all sorts of healing centres and holistic approaches which I would probably never have encountered if I had stayed in my previous home.

Another decade went by and again I knew it was time to move from my home on the north side (being both an astrologer and numerologist I tend to work things out in advance!). This time I was certain I wanted to leave Dublin but had little idea where to go. Because I don't have a regular 'day job' I was lucky enough to be able to drive around Ireland and see where I would like to live. The only restriction I put on myself was to ensure it was less than 150 kilometres from Dublin so that I could commute for media purposes should that be necessary. Of course I asked my angels to come along with me on my travels and, having checked out properties on the south-east and the south-midlands, one day I decided to go north-east and look at a property which was on the market. I did so, hated the property on sight, but continued driving north and then, on a whim, turned west. I was making my way back to Dublin when I came to the small town of Virginia, which is in the Lake District here, and I had an overwhelming urge to have a cup of coffee. So I parked the car and discovered I was outside an estate agent's! Deciding this was too much of a 'coincidence' to overlook (or more likely angelic synchronicity!),

I went into the agency and asked for the list of houses for sale. The first house on the list is the one I bought and currently own. Another little experience of angel magic!

Inviting Angel Magic into Your Life

You are possibly thinking that the sorts of experiences mentioned above can only happen to someone like me, but that isn't the case. Do bear in mind that angels want to be our close friends, not some distant formal beings far out of reach. So treat them as friends. Invite your angel along with you, whatever you are doing, just as you would a friend. Be open. Practise openness every day and get into the habit of looking around you and noticing things like scent in the air. Angels are 'beings of light', so it is a good idea to light a candle for your angel in your home as a conscious decision to invite your angel to be with you. Then, each time you look at the candle flame you will be reminded that you are never alone. And if you drive a car, clear up the passenger seat or the rear seat and make room for your angelic companion.

Angel Experiences

Angels can help us in every area of our life, be it in relationships with authority, family, lovers, friends or strangers. As Pope Pious XI said: 'Whenever we have to speak with someone who is rather closed to our argument and with whom, therefore, the conversation needs to be very persuasive, we go to our guardian angel.' They won't, however, do the work necessary in order to sort matters out, they will give us the guidance needed in order to do it ourselves. That is what angel magic is all about!

I was amused and pleased to see in two recent films, both of which involved angels, *The Preacher's Wife* and *City of Angels*, that there were two very strong points made within them. Point one is that angels are here to give us guidance, and point two is that they cannot make us take it! So, again, we are all given at least one angel but we are also given free will, and that latter gift can sometimes prove to be a double-edged sword!

Recently someone asked me 'Margaret, how do you get people to believe in angels?' I replied immediately, 'I don't'. And it's true. It's not my job as I see it to persuade you that angels exist – that is up to the angels. My mission is to help you connect with them and so bring their magic into your life. Some

people offer the service of communing with your angel and passing on its messages. My belief is that you should commune with your own angel. Getting in touch with angels is no secret. All you need do is be open, ask for help, and take your angel's advice. That's how you invite angel magic into your life.

Within the next pages there are many rituals and exercises you can practise which will help you make daily contact. Just for now, though, these are the secrets to getting in touch with angels.

Inviting angel magic into your life is easy. All you need to do is be open, ask for help, and take your angel's advice.

Getting in Touch with Your Angels

1. Keep your eyes, ears and heart open to receive messages in whichever way they are meant to come to you, for example, through a friend, through a stranger, through just 'happening' to turn on the radio/TV and hearing someone give the answer you are looking for.

2. Accept the fact that your angel is with you at this moment. Close your eyes and ask your angel to give you some form of proof that it is with you now. It could just be a feeling of warmth, a change in the energy around you, a certain 'knowing' that you are never alone from this moment on.

3. Say the following little 'prayer':

Angels of love, beings of light,
please bring enlightenment to me here and now.
Help me to bring magic into my life
so that I can share it with others.
Help me to fill my heart with love
so that I can share it with others.
Fill my heart with light and love as I speak to you now.

4. Get into the habit of taking a few moments to yourself and your angel every day. Each time you are in a queue

or stuck in a traffic jam, spend those precious moments communing together.

Enjoy your enhanced quality of life now you know your angel is with you.

Chapter 3

Daily Contact with Angels

How to Get in Contact with Your Angels

It's often difficult to remember that the angels are always with us, especially if you spend your day rushing about attempting to do a hundred different tasks and trying to keep everyone happy! Believe me, if you give yourself a few minutes in the morning, preferably before you leap out of bed, to connect with your angels and ask for their guidance for the day ahead, you will manage

to dispense with a lot of unnecessary pressure and feel much happier by the time you go to bed that night. So how do you get the help you need?

'Silence is the language of the angels' as they say, so when you want to connect with your angel do try to find a place of silence. It is always a good idea to light a candle too, which is simply a conscious decision to bring light into your life – after all, the angels are 'beings of light'. Watching a candle flame for a few moments is also a very simple and direct way to bring you back to the 'centre' of your being, or as others term it 'into the now', and help you to leave all the cares and irritations of the outer world behind you.

The following meditation exercise will show you how to connect with your angel. If you don't usually practise any form of meditation, it is a very simple exercise to follow. The reason for meditating, or doing what I call 'a visualization exercise', is to help you get reconnected with the 'real you' which is your spiritual core. When you do this you should find it easy to contact your angel who is, after all, a being from the spiritual world.

It is helpful to bear in mind that we are about 95% spirit which is enveloped in a physical body that keeps us grounded to Earth, so contacting that 95% should be easy. However, often our ego, which is part of the remaining 'human' aspect of us, can kick up a fuss if it feels it is losing our attention. It may act like a little child, throwing a tantrum and causing problems until it gets our attention. If so, treat it like that small, fearful child. Talk to it, console it, be gentle with it. Fighting and ignoring it will not make it disappear! By treating it gently it will let go of the fear that is making it overreact in the first place. If I find my 'mind' is acting up when I want to meditate, I just speak to it saying 'I'm going on a short break and I'll be back in a while.' Just like placating a child! With a little bit of practice the act of meditating or enjoying a 'guided visualization' will come easily to you.

In the following exercise, you may also get to learn the name of your angel. Personally, I don't really believe that angels have names as we know the meaning of the term, for they don't need them. I do understand, however, that it is important for us to have a name to cling to sometimes, to make an angel's

presence more 'normal' for us, and it is easier for us to communicate with others when we have a name to identify them. Of course, the scholars of old would have needed to have names in order to put angels into hierarchical classifications. Maybe they are right, but to me we are all equal in the eyes of God and so are our angels. Having said that, I do now know the names my angels go by and it is very easy to find yours. If you don't get a name for your angel during the following exercise, don't worry. A name will surface within the next few days that tends to stick in your mind, or keeps being repeated. This is the angels synchronizing events so that you will 'get the message'.

In my own case, while I was very aware of one angel in particular in my life, it wasn't until quite recently when I was reading a book by an American on angels that I actually asked for its name. Up till then, working alone with my angel, it had never occurred to me to find out! I was sitting at my PC in my office (not the place I would usually recommend!) and I closed my eyes while I asked for its name. Into my ear came what I believed was 'Laura' and I immediately responded with the thought that this is my niece's name and I must be imagining it!

But as I still kept my eyes shut I saw 'in my mind's eye' a view of a garden and it was as though my angel was hanging up big, square, white terrycloth nappies on the washing line with the separate letters L-O-R-I-E-L printed on each one. So the name wasn't 'Laura', it was 'Loriel'. Loriel is who I consider to be my guardian angel, while I have several others who help me in other areas of my life, such as business, technology, painting and gardening, and so on. Though angels don't have a gender, I always think of Loriel as a female energy. It is possible that your angel's name may come to you in an extraordinary place, but more likely that you will receive it if you meditate as follows.

Visualization Exercise: Meditating with Your Angel

It's essential that you are comfortable and in a sitting position rather than lying down (for when you lie down you may fall asleep!), and that you are as relaxed as possible. Make sure there will be no interruptions, so unplug the phone and turn off your mobile! You may like to play some soothing music in the background. If you wish you can record the following exercise in your own voice onto an audiocassette.

(If you do so, try to time it so that it lasts 15–20 minutes.) You can change the word 'you' to 'I' if you wish.

Always begin the visualization exercises in this book by connecting yourself with the Earth. That is simply imagining yourself with tiny little roots or magnets coming from the soles of your feet and connecting into the Earth below. This will keep you grounded throughout the exercise.

When you have done this, simply close your eyes and continue to breathe deeply for a few moments. Try to imagine as you breathe in that you are inhaling golden light into your lungs. Gold is the colour of the angels.

Now, as you breathe the golden light into your two lungs, you can see it spreading all the way around your body as though it's moving through your blood vessels. It's moving into your feet, around the toes and up into your ankles. It's moving up your lower legs into your shins and calves and now it's filling up your knees. The golden light is moving up your thighs and into your hips, helping you to stand up for yourself and cut ties with the past. It's moving into your lower body, helping you to release what needs to be released. Now it's spreading upwards into your heart and your lungs and into your chest. All the while the golden light is moving around your body you are breathing out fears, negativity and old behaviour patterns. As the golden light moves into your shoulders it releases any burdens you are carrying. And now it moves down your spine all the way to the base of your backbone, strengthening and healing any aspect of your life where support is the issue. The golden light is now healing and strengthening your support system. And now it spreads down your shoulders, into your arms and into your hands. And as it moves into your two hands it helps you to give and receive in perfect balance. Now the golden light moves into your throat and your neck, up into your head, under your scalp and under all of your skin, releasing fears and renewing your inner strength. Now you know that you are becoming filled with light and therefore finding it easier to connect with your angel. Enjoy the knowledge that you are filled with golden light!

Now hold your left hand open on your heart. Allow any inter-fering thoughts to come into your mind and then leave your mind, and when you feel you have attained silence simply ask in your mind the question, 'Angel, what is your name?' The very first name that occurs to you is the one for your angel.

With your hand still on your heart, ask 'Is there anything I need to know right now?' and await a reply. It may come in a spoken message, or it may just be a definite feeling you undergo. Whichever way it comes it is a message for you at this moment.

When you feel the time is right, take a deep breath into your lungs and now, as you breathe out, you can once more feel your fin-gers and your toes. Again, you breathe in deeply and now, as you breathe out, you can once more feel your whole body from the top of your head to the tips of your toes. And now, as you take another deep breath in and out, it's time to open your eyes and return to this place, feeling refreshed, relaxed and better than before.

Did you receive a name? Record the name immediately. During the next few days and weeks call your angel by this name and see how close you feel. You may have received a very simple everyday name. Should this be the case, don't be disappointed. You were given a simple, everyday name because your angel wants you to connect with it in a simple, everyday fashion! If the name seems completely unacceptable to you, redo the exercise and ask again. And bear in mind you can have more than one angel, so if you get two or three names this means you have two or three angels looking after you.

Record also any message you may have received, making sure you use the precise words you heard. One of the first messages I recorded was 'There is good reason to love yourself.' If I had left it to memory alone, I would possibly have written down 'Love yourself' or 'We love you,' which are different messages to the one I received. When I thought about the message in the following weeks and months, and I remember this was the time when I was going through a very bad patch, that precise message made me wonder 'What reason have I to love myself?' I couldn't think of a

thing, yet I did know that if my angels thought there was a good reason to love myself they had to be right. So the answer came back to me that my problems arose from not loving myself – from trying to be someone else in order to gain others' approval. When I finally 'got the message' that somewhere along the way I must have done something right, after all the angels said so, then I began to slowly (very slowly!) change my opinion of myself.

Connecting with your angels is simple. Keeping yourself aware of them in your daily life, and therefore enjoying their magic, needs just a little effort from you. Your angels are with you at all times, but they cannot force you to be aware of them, nor can they force you to follow their guidance. Working alongside your angel to bring magic into your life is a collaborative process. It doesn't take much effort, just a willingness to be open. Here are some rituals to help you connect with your angels and bring their magic into your daily life.

Connecting with your angels is simple. Keeping yourself aware of them in your daily life, and therefore enjoying their magic, needs just a little effort from you.

Rituals for Connecting with Your Angels

Whenever you are enjoying an angelic ritual, try to make sure that you won't be interrupted by people or phones or external noise. Set aside some special time to yourself every day or every week, and don't let any outside demands intrude on that specific time. Play some undemanding music if you wish, be silent, or laugh and sing if you prefer. Some of the rituals in this book you could even share with like-minded companions, or your children. The main thing is that you focus on what you are doing with love and joy.

An Everyday Ritual

A simple way to ensure you receive angelic help every day in your life is to wake up and say the following before you even

get out of bed. Say it aloud when you can, remembering the magic of the spoken word:

'The Angel of Divine Love goes before me and prepares my way.'

When you look at that statement you can see that you are asking your angel to go ahead of you through the day and prepare the road for you. As always, your angel is here to help you, not to do your work for you! So your road will be prepared for you, not cleared of what we may consider to be 'obstacles'. Instead, the road will be made ready for you to learn as much as possible from every experience you encounter. And remember, your angel is with you so you are not alone. I find that short statement very helpful when facing some difficult situations, whether it is ringing up the bank manager and requesting a loan, or being supportive to someone in dire need. Whatever it is you are facing, with the Angel of Divine Love preparing the way for you, you cannot but succeed!

The following two rituals are creative exercises you can carry out on your own or with like-minded companions. They are fun, too, so perhaps you could even invite children to join in.

A Ritual for Focussing on What You want in Life

As I mentioned earlier, the written or spoken word holds huge power, and the following exercise will help you to focus on what you truly seek in your life. Do remember the power it holds, so don't ask for anything you can't or don't want to handle!

Making a Magic Circle

To make this Mandala (which means 'magic circle') all you will need is a sheet of plain paper (approximately A4 size) and felt-tip pens, crayons or paints. Don't worry, you don't have to be an artist to do this, though if you do feel totally incompetent you can always ask archangel Gabriel, who looks after creativity, to give you a helping hand. I like to keep things informal between me and my angels, after all they are my friends, so I would say: *'Angel Gabriel, please guide my hand as I try to express myself...'* You could be amazed at what you achieve!

Here is how you make the magic circle. Draw a large circle on the full page and divide it into four equal sections: the section at the top is the north; the section at the bottom is the south; the west section is to the left, and the east section is to the right. The north is symbolic of spiritual needs; the south is symbolic of physical needs; the west is symbolic of intuitive, emotional and creative needs, and the east is symbolic of mental attitude, learning and philosophy.

Now draw some symbols in each of the four sections of the things you want to bring into your life with angel magic. They can be anything and everything from the physical to the ephemeral: love, harmony, companionship and sexual compatibility would go in the west section, while money and abundance would go in the south section, and patience, easy learning, intuition and knowledge would go in the east section ... the list is endless. Rather than write the words down, instead draw the symbol, such as books for learning, cats for psychic ability, the glyphs for Venus and Mars for sexual compatibility, angels for spiritual guidance, gold bullion for wealth, and so on. What you want is up to you, so trust yourself. I would put things like a lighted candle (for enlightenment!) and books in the east for learning, a heart, flowers, rings, two matchstick people in the west for emotional support, and so forth. The main thing is not to be too formal. Make it fun, make it bright – allow your mind to wander while your creative instinct comes to the fore. Most of all, enjoy the ritual! And remember, now you have committed yourself to having these things in your life they are going to appear 'like magic' – though not necessarily overnight!

Now sign the mandala, put the date on it, and you can either put it away in a private place or hang it on the wall to remind yourself just how many magical things are on their way into your life.

A RITUAL FOR ANGELIC INSPIRATION

Over the years I have received many messages from my own angels and kept a record of them. Usually the messages would come to me in the middle of the night when I was deeply asleep

and I would waken to write them down, then return to sleep. (By the way, 4am or thereabouts is the most psychic time of your sleep. If you begin to wake up unexpectedly at this time on occasion, don't worry. It's just a message saying your angels are getting in touch. Do keep a pad and pen handy so that you can write down any messages you may receive, no matter how odd they may appear at the time.) Sometimes the words would be a direct answer to a query in my mind, while at other times I would get the 'answer' before I even asked the 'question' shortly afterwards. Just proving again that the angels live in the magical space of 'angel time', knowing exactly what is on the cards for me, no matter how slow I might be in picking up on the situation.

When I was told by them to give a course called 'Talking With Angels', which set me off on my mission in 1994, I didn't have a clue as to how to even start such a thing, let alone continue it. I did have the sense to ask their advice, of course, and I was 'angelically inspired' to use the messages I had been given by them over the intervening years. I later printed the messages and made them into 'Angel Inspiration Cards'. Whenever I feel

lost or unsure of what I am doing, I simply shuffle the pack and pick an 'inspiration'. It's amazing just how accurate the answer can be.

You can bring angel magic into your life by doing something similar. To begin with you may like to use some of the messages I have collected over the years (see pages 75–8), but as you become closer and more open to your angel's guidance, you can also record the messages you receive and make them into your own Inspiration Cards.

Making Angel Inspiration Cards

As I mentioned earlier, the French word 'espeler' means 'to read out' and this later came into the English language as the word 'spell' which means 'to name the letters of a word'. Of course we now take the word 'spell' as being both a method of using letters to form a word as well as a method of creating magic. As noted before, words hold their own power. We are what we say we are, we are what we think we are. So think carefully about each word as you write it and as you say it aloud.

Make the creation of your Angel Inspiration Cards a special ritual. Invite someone special to join you if you wish, or else just ask your angel to be with you. If you have children, perhaps you could encourage them to make their own cards, too, or else to help you.

All you will need to make your Inspiration cards is some cardboard or heavy paper (white or coloured, the choice is yours), scissors or a stanley knife, a writing instrument (or a packet of felt-tip pens in different colours), and perhaps some glitter and glue to make them specially 'angelic'. Cut the material into handy cards of the same size and write out your chosen messages. Be as creative as possible, perhaps even using gold ink, always remembering that the colour gold is the symbol of angels. (Although you can buy ready-cut card and type out the messages, the actual ritual of cutting and writing gives your special cards extra power.)

Here are some examples of my own Angel Inspiration Cards:

You, alone, are enough.

Do not whisper your name, we know it well.

Find your strength in love.

Trust comes from within.
The only one you need to trust is yourself.

Within each of our spirits there is our Self and many angels.

Do not search for us, we have already found you.

Angels speak to those who silence their
minds long enough to hear.

Open your heart to the sound of silence and you shall hear
the wonders of all that exist.

Open your heart to angel love.

Know only that you are loved.

God doesn't ask us to be perfect,
God asks us only to be present.

Angels take note of everything we do.
(The angels have noted your good deeds.)

Be not afraid.

Watch out, there's an angel about!

We are born to walk with angels,
but instead we search for jewels in the mud.

Angels know your good bits and your bad bits,
and they still love you.

You're never alone, you've an angel!

Love yourself, live the moment.

You are the Light Bearer.
(Share your increasing knowledge and enlighten others.)

Listen, it's the voice of your angel.

Celebrate this day! (Concern yourself only with today).

Silence is the language of the angels.

Those who walk with angels learn to soar above the clouds.

Be attentive to your angel and listen to its voice.

Be patient. All will be revealed in Angel Time.

Prepare for a miracle!

Your voice is my voice. (Speak up on behalf of your angel.)

There is good reason to love yourself.

Look at the wonders around you!

Some other messages you could make if you want a simple answer are:

Yes

No

Wait

When you have made these Inspiration Cards you may like to keep them in a special box or a little bag which you find particularly attractive, or even make a special holder for yourself. Remember they hold magic within them, so treat them with respect! Start the day with a message and choose one whenever you are in need of special help. Before shuffling the pack and choosing a card, take yourself into a moment of silence, ask your angel to help you choose the right answer, then pick one without looking at the message first. Trust your instinct! You will be amazed at how accurate and supportive the messages are when you use them to help you in the future. Using these cards on a daily basis is a simple and enjoyable way to remind ourselves, and especially children, how easy it is to keep in touch with our angels.

Chapter 4

The Angels of nature

'Only through the communions with the Angels of the Heavenly Father will we learn to see the unseen, to hear that which cannot be heard, and to speak the unspoken word,' Jesus of Nazareth explained, according to the Gospel of the Essenes. He went on to say that we should communicate with 12 angels in order to 'do as Angels do'. These are the angels of the Sun, Water, Air, Earth, Life, Joy, Power, Love, Wisdom, Eternal Life, Work and Peace.

The Angels of Nature

It is not so surprising that Jesus states that all the elements of our planet, and our lives, have an angel looking after them. As it says in the Talmud, the body of Jewish law and legend dating back thousands of years, 'Every blade of grass has its own angel that bends over it and whispers "Grow! Grow!"' The more we understand that we, and even every blade of grass, are each part of a mosaic which makes up all our lives, the more easily we can let go of the need to control, and so open up to angelic guidance. In this way, not only will our lives be healthier, so will our planet.

It is only in relatively recent years that we seem to have assumed we are the only creations on the Earth who are blessed with angels and other help from nature's kingdom. Some people tend to treat animals, insects and plant life as something to be abused rather than honoured. Yet the more we treat our planet with respect, the healthier and more balanced we will all become. Some believe that the Fourth Commandment 'Honour thy father and thy mother' originally meant 'Honour thy Father Sky (and all things that come down from heaven such as angels) and thy Mother Earth.' The

ancient pagans, whose culture and traditions have been frowned upon for many years, seemed to understand the need for balance in everything that they did much more than our generations. They looked up to the sky for guidance from the stars and the position of the Sun and the Moon, and they honoured the earth with regular rituals. The word 'pagan' means 'of the earth' and they, being a pastoral community, recognized the importance of keeping harmony between nature and humanity. They have passed on to us many rituals based on their belief system, but most people follow the motions without understanding why.

Some Ancient Rituals

Every year as Christmas approaches (which of course is the time of the Winter Solstice in the Northern Hemisphere) we bring sprigs of holly, ivy and a tree into our homes. Why? The age-old reason is so that the 'sprites' of nature will enter our homes, along with this greenery, in order to be protected from the cold and the frosts of winter. Because of this protection from the elements, it was believed that the beings of the devic kingdom (the angels that look after the Earth and all that grows on it) would then return to the outdoors in Spring to look after our budding crops and gardens. It's still innate in us to follow this and other rituals, yet how many of us question why we do so?

Even the Christian festival of Easter, which is symbolized by eggs and bunny rabbits, originates from pagan festivities. The actual word 'Easter' originates from 'Eostre', which was an ancient Anglo-Saxon festival to honour the Goddess of Spring of the same name, who was also the Fertility Goddess. The date chosen was the first Full Moon following the Spring Equinox. Then the Christian Church, which liked to develop their own festivals around the ancient rites, chose to celebrate their own 'rebirth' of their leader at the same time. Each year the Christian festival of Easter is on the first Sunday after the first Full Moon after the Spring Equinox, and when Christian missionaries took their beliefs to the Southern Hemisphere, Easter automatically followed the first Full Moon after the Autumn Equinox in those lands. The goddess Eostre was symbolized by the hare and the egg, and it's amazing to realize we still keep to those old traditions. So on Easter Sunday when you crack open that chocolate egg, you will know where the practice came from!

There is no need to be frightened of 'pagan' rituals – they are just rites which are connected with our pastoral heritage. And our ancestors knew more about the 'meaning of life' than we do!

Anyone who works in harmony with Mother Earth will already realize that they are not alone in their task. What we call 'green fingers' is really a gift from nature. It is because they honour the earth and try their utmost not to abuse it that they benefit from an ensuing abundance not only of flowers, plants or crops, but also the gain of birdsong and seed spread, bees' help in pollination and enhanced beauty, peace and serenity in their environment.

I cannot change the planet overnight, and nor can you. However, each of us can change and heal our own little patch of soil, whether it's a single window box or ten acres of meadow, and we can do so with the help of our angels. The power of devic help when working with, rather than against, the natural kingdom is proven in the following story.

Each of us can change and heal our own little patch of soil, whether it's a single window box or ten acres of meadow, and we can do so with the help of our angels.

The Miracle Garden

In 1962 a small group of people came together and set up a community in Findhorn Bay, Moray, Scotland. There they lived in mobile accommodation on the seaward sand dunes and the following year one member of the community, Peter Caddy, began to sow the first seeds in what was to become the abundant 'Findhorn Garden', an experiment of man, devas and nature spirits all working together.

Despite the fact that conifers planted on the neighbouring sand dunes took 50 years to make the ground tough enough to allow grass to grow on them, and while the only other vegetation was gorse and broom, Peter Caddy and his extended family succeeded in growing a variety of vegetables, fruit and herbs within the next few years. They began with radishes and lettuces, and during their first season grew 65 different vegetables,

21 different kinds of fruit and 42 different herbs. As time went on they also planted trees and hedges.

How did they achieve such magical abundance? By listening to and following the advice they received from the angelic realm. New Age nonsense? No, their extraordinary work has been acknowledged by many scientists involved in various areas of horticulture. Peter Caddy believes that devas are the angelic beings who supervise growth of all the species in the plant kingdom as well as wind, colour, sound, etc, while it is the nature sprites who do the actual work of ensuring sap is rising, and so on. So it's a co-operative effort between man who sows, the devas who supervise the overall environment for growth and the nature sprites who do the 'work'. It certainly brought about magic for him!

Sir George Trevelyan, Bt., who is a member of the Soil Association and an advocate of working in union with the devic kingdom, says there are four simple methods of invoking the help of devas in order that we can all enjoy the fruits of a healthier, abundant natural world:

1. Acknowledge that devas exist and offer our love and thanks.

2. Invoke their aid in inner thought contact by recognizing their presence and communicating with them either silently through thought or else speaking aloud.

3. Listen with alert attention. Don't necessarily expect to hear an answer, but allow yourself to be guided by what feels right. Take note of what doesn't work and don't make the mistake again!

4. Give thanks with love from the heart.

Living in Harmony with the Earth

I have always been interested in ecological issues. Some years ago I went to a spirit guide channeller and asked if there was any way we could help to heal places such as Chernobyl in Belarus, which was so devastated by the nuclear fuel tank explosion in the late 1980s. I was told that if we ask the angels of the earth to cleanse and renew the soil it would begin slowly to be healed and so be able once again to feed its people. The

Angel of Rebirth is Amatiel who looks after Springtime and any area of our life which is about renewal, rebirth and new beginnings. If you know of any tract of land which needs healing, especially after disastrous pollution, ask the angel Amatiel to be with you as you visualize new life coming back to the soil.

I have heard it said that the reason for the birds' 'Dawn Chorus' is that the vibrations they make in their song are telling the earth to get to work and help the vegetation to grow, while at sunset they sing again to tell it to rest in its work. It sounds like a very sensible explanation to me and I often wonder what would occur if birdsong was introduced to a barren area of land. What with the help of the birds and some angels, it couldn't fail to thrive!

Because we never had an 'industrial revolution' in Ireland, very little building of either housing estates or factories ever went on until the last two or three decades except in the major cities. Because of this, and because the art of storytelling has been so strong for many centuries, there is a great respect for sacred wells (found where the whitethorn grows) and 'fairy rings' (circular outcrops of earth or stone, often of different texture to the surrounding land). There are some roads built on 'fairy land' and locals tell that many accidents occur in these areas because the county council built despite the fairy ring. My own father would not touch a fairy ring in our farm and warned us as children never to go near it, and even now many fields have small patches of land which are never touched by farm machinery. The respect which the Findhorn settlers showed the land in Scotland was repaid by abundant crops. Show respect, too, and see how your harvest will increase with a little angel magic!

When you accept that every blade of grass really does have an angel looking after it, you could become quite paranoid about standing on grass, cutting flowers, eating fruit and vegetables and, of course, destroying weeds! That is quite a natural response, but there is no need to continue it for long. In order to work in harmony with the Earth, all you need do is speak to the devas and ask their permission to make the necessary changes, or tell them in advance what you are going to do. Treat them with respect and they will return the compliment. There is a ritual following later in this chapter which will help you and your angel heal the Earth and help it grow prosperous.

Your Own Miracle Garden

What do you need to ensure plant life will thrive? Earth, air, water and sunshine. And the added help of the angels, of course. Naturally it would be better if you could find an alternative to using pesticides and chemical fertilizers, but even if you are gardening organically, you need to consult with the beings in your garden first before taking any action. Yes, this might seem crazy, but if you consider all the little beings living there, it is very unfair to suddenly obliterate them simply because you want to grow a pretty flower or two! Remember the 'balance of nature' is part of the magic that will help your garden blossom, so go outside and either speak aloud or just in your thoughts, but first of all tell them what you want to achieve, then explain that you need them to move away, if necessary, while you make the changes.

It is also vital to understand that every living thing that grows has not only a right to grow but also a reason for that growth. That includes what we call 'weeds', too! While some people spend their days getting rid of dandelions, they are forgetting that each part of that plant can be used positively, for instance, the leaves in salad, the flowers in wine. Why would they exist if they didn't have a reason for being here? The dandelion flower is the symbol of the Sun. Look at it when it flowers and see how many insects thrive on its existence. Everything is life and we are simply part of life, not all of it. So if you don't want to grow dandelions ask the devas to take their seeds elsewhere so that they can grow naturally where there is space for them without fear of obliteration by us. Also, if you really have to kill off weeds, do so before they come into flower. It is also important to leave a patch of garden to grow wild and undisturbed. The gardeners of old always did this because they knew the importance of 'balance' in nature.

When you work in the garden it is important that you work with joy in your thoughts and actions. Remember you are in the process of co-creation with the other beings there. Sing, laugh, work with others, speak to the angels, speak to the flowers, plants, trees, bees and the birds. I have noticed recently how many birds have joined me in my garden and even in my house on occasion. (Not a good idea for them with my two cats,

however!) When nature accepts you and welcomes you into their realm, take it as a very big compliment that you are doing the right things. Have as much colour as possible, for colour gives off healthy vibrations, and the addition of bells or chimes also brings the vibration of sound. Without needing to know the intricacies of such vibrations and how they help the energy flow, it simply feels wonderful for us humans to be in a place surrounded by sound and colour, and as the angels are 'beings of light' they will appreciate it even more. Make or buy some little angel figurines which you can 'plant' around your garden. If you enjoy being creative you could make your own little angels with modelling clay and get friends or children to help. Be as creative as you wish, bringing joy and fun into what you do. The garden will then reflect back to you all the good things you have given it. Spending time working in the garden 'because you have to' is most detrimental to both you and the garden itself. How can plant life blossom and show itself at its best if it has been put there by unwilling hands? Don't be surprised if it goes into a huff and wilts on you!

The Angels of Nature

Be as creative as you wish, bringing joy and fun into what you do. The garden will then reflect back to you all the good things you have given it.

When I was four years old I planted some lettuce seeds and diligently watered them and cared for them. Then we had to go away suddenly due to a family emergency and returned two weeks later to find what remained of some very dead-looking lettuce shoots. Though my family said they would never grow again and I was wasting my time, I tended to them regardless. I was very in tune with nature and the angels so I used to go down to the lettuces and talk to them every day and tell them how important they were to me. Sure enough, they recovered and grew into very abundant plants which we duly ingested.

My last two homes had large untended gardens when I moved in and they became my priority. Over the years I know that the devas and sprites were delighted when I looked after them. My current garden is more of a half-acre field, and in the few months since I've been living in my new home I've managed to transform at least some of it from a virtual desert into a

bright, colourful and abundant garden. Before I act I commune with the devas first and ask them what I should do, and I tell them in advance when I am going to cut the grass or weed the area. When I gather weeds I put them towards compost, and I do feel this recycling of unwanted growth is appreciated by the nature beings. With all the new house building going on nowadays, I feel my job is to grow things that encourage birds, bees, butterflies and other wildlife. Despite the fact that the soil is stony and apparently poor, I have abundant lavender, heather, roses, fuchsia, lilac ... the list goes on. I am also growing lots of peas, rhubarb, lettuce, cabbage and broccoli ... and have planted over 100 trees. So don't give up if you have only got a patch of stony ground or if your seedlings aren't growing. Ask the angels what you should be doing differently and take their advice. Treat the new growth tenderly and tell it how much you appreciate its presence. You can say it silently in your mind if you feel foolish, but just do it! That is what the people at Findhorn did and the results were miraculous!

Help from the Nature Angels

Archangel Uriel looks after the planet and when you are working in your garden call on him to come and give guidance and protection to whatever you plant there. Call on the Angel of Life, the Angel of Joy and the Angel of Earth to bless your garden. Call on the angel Arias if you want to grow sweet smelling herbs, and if you are thinking of having a water feature, ask angel Ariel along. This angel will also help to keep your garden moist so you don't need to fear drought. There are other angels who are responsible for the different seasons. The more you are aware of them, the more you include them in your daily thoughts and thank them for their help, the better your garden will grow! Check out the 'Angels of the Calendar Year' section in Chapter 1 and work with the angel of the current month. The following will help you to connect more closely with the angels of the seasons.

Note: Because the seasons are experienced differently in the Southern Hemisphere, I have included dates for both hemispheres.

THE ANGEL OF SPRING - AMATIEL

As the days begin to grow longer, ask the angel Amatiel to come into your garden, and perhaps you could put something special there in order to honour this angel's arrival. Amatiel is the Angel of Spring, who has quite a hard job helping plant life break through the cold ground and encouraging it back to life! When you talk to Amatiel, or any other angel, try to be informal in your approach and treat the conversation as though you were chatting with a friend, for that's what an angel is. What would you say to a friend who was working hard breaking up the frozen soil in order to bring growth, colour and health back into your life?

Visualization Exercise: A Ritual for the Spring Equinox

March 20–23 (Northern Hemisphere);
September 20–23 (Southern Hemisphere)

Carry out this visualization exercise indoors. You might like to record it in your own voice first or, if in a group situation, get one person to read it out. It should take between 15–20 minutes. Remember you can change the word 'you' to 'I' if

---

you wish. Wear or surround yourself with anything coloured gold, orange or bright yellow – the brighter the better! If you burn incense, choose a Spring scent such as jasmine. As always, you should be in a comfortable sitting position, rather than lying down.

Before starting this visualization exercise, imagine there are tiny roots coming out through the soles of your feet and connecting you to the Earth below. This will keep you grounded throughout the exercise. When you have done this and you are in a comfortable position, take a deep breath. And then, as you breathe in again, imagine there's a beautiful white light travelling up your toes, across your feet and into your ankles. And as you breathe out, allow any tension in this area to gently flow out into the ground below.

As you breathe in again, the beautiful white light travels up from your ankles into your calves, and moves up into your knees. And as you breathe out, allow any tension in this area to gently flow out into the ground below.

Now breathe in the white light and feel it rise into your upper torso. See the white light travel into your heart and into your lungs. And as you breathe out, allow any tension in this area to gently flow out into the ground below.

And as you breathe in, the beautiful white light moves up into your shoulders, releasing any knots and tension there. It flows gently down into your upper arms, your lower arms, and into your fingertips. And as you breathe out, any tension in this area gently flows down into the ground below.

Now, as you breathe in again, the beautiful white light travels up into your throat and into your neck. The white light releases any blocks in your throat and you find it easier to express yourself creatively. And now the white light moves up into the back of your head, and as you breathe out, any tension here gently flows out into the ground below.

As you breathe in, watch as the white light moves up into your ears, and it moves into your chin and your mouth, and into your nose, and up into your eyes and your forehead; and now it goes all the way under your scalp and up into the crown of your

head. And as you breathe out, any tension here gently flows into the ground below. And you know that the earth will recycle anything you have exhaled and turn it into light.

You know now that you are filled from the tips of your toes to the top of your head with pure white healing light. And as you gently breathe in and out you feel healing take place all over your body, and in particular in any place where there is a blockage of energy. How wonderful it is to be filled with healing white light. How happy and content you feel!

Now I want you to imagine that you are in a country place, standing on the top of a small hill. As you look around you you see that far in the distance are mountain peaks. What a beautiful sight they are. And now you look below and see a green valley. How relaxing the green seems, and how quiet it is. All you can hear is birdsong and the sound of my voice. You feel completely relaxed and at peace as you look around you. And as you raise your head you see a clear blue sky above, and feel the gentle healing rays of the Sun touch your skin. Breathe in the freshness of the country air. How good it feels!

And now you look down at your feet and see you are reaching into the earth. There is nothing to fear; you are happy to be in touch with the earth. The soil is soft and warm. You know you are rooted in it, perfectly safe, perfectly calm. Now as you breathe in you can feel the energy of the earth coming into you. It's as though you have a stem instead of a body and the energy is travelling upwards, making you feel refreshed and strong. Now the energy is moving into your limbs. You realize now you are like a beautiful flower, growing tall and strong. Feel the energy move into your limbs – it's as though they have become soft, delicate petals. The energy is filling them with joy and love. You want to open up to joy and love, so you open your petals. Now you see what flower you have become.

It's a wonderful feeling being a flower. You can feel the soft delicacy of the petals, and you can feel the strength of your leaves and stem. Now you can feel a gentle raindrop land on one of your petals and you feel a sense of joy at its touch. The gentle breeze blows and you can feel yourself moving with the breeze, as though you are dancing. Everything around you is alive. Look

around you. Feel how wonderful it is to be this flower, surrounded by other beings of nature.

Look closely. Perhaps you can see some of the 'shining ones', the angels of nature. Can you converse with them? Ask them if there is anything you can do to improve their environment. Can you sense how gentle and loving they are? Spend time with them. Now thank them for being with you.

It's time to leave this beautiful place behind you, but you know you can always return whenever you want to be in touch with the beauty of nature. Take a deep breath into both your lungs and now, as you breathe out, you can once more feel your fingers and your toes. Take another deep breath into both your lungs and now, as you breathe out, you can feel your body from top to toe. With a final deep breath into both lungs, you now know as you breathe out that you are completely back in your body, in this room and it is time to open your eyes. Now you feel happy, fulfilled and at one with your world.

THE ANGEL OF SUMMER - ANGEL TUBIEL

The angel Tubiel will enhance your garden with an abundance of blossoms and fruit during the Summer months. In order to ensure a perfect balance of rain and sunshine, ask the angel Matriel and the angel Moriel to enter your garden to bring it into balance. Matriel is the Angel of Rain, and it is Moriel who looks after the wind. Sometimes we need a little wind to either blow the rain clouds away, or to bring them to us. Again, speak to these angels as though you were speaking to a friend. Ask them to visit your garden in order to bring about perfect growth for yourself and every being involved in it.

A Ritual for Summer Solstice

June 20–23 (Northern Hemisphere);

December 20–23 (Southern Hemisphere)

If at all possible it would be best to carry out this ceremony by a running water course, such as a river, canal or a stream, but if this isn't possible improvise in your own home! Perhaps you could play an audio tape of a flowing stream in the background to help you imagine yourself there. All you

will need for this special ritual is a white candle for each person present, some white paper and a pencil (and a large bowl of water if indoors). If you burn incense, choose a summer scent such as rose or lavender.

The Summer Solstice celebrates the middle of the pastoral year. Gardens, parks and farmlands should be bursting with healthy growth. After all the hard work since Spring we can now see the benefits around us. It is a time to thank the angels and devic beings for the gift of life.

Whether alone or among friends, spend some time focussing on what you have to celebrate within your own life and invite your angel to join you. Have you forged a new friend-ship? Enjoyed romance? Developed a positive thinking pattern? Conceived a child? Been introduced to your angel? Developed a new career? Or do you just feel fulfilled and joyful? Now consider what you wish to achieve in the next few weeks which remain of Summer.

When you are ready, bless the candles, then light them. Write down on the white paper your thanks for what you have, and your wishes for the coming Autumn. Shape the paper into a boat, which can later be cast onto the water. (Improvise at home with a bowl of water or by filling the sink or bath – or keep your prayer boats until you can set them free on a running water course.)

Now spend some time in silence bringing into your imagination the image, the feeling, the knowledge of your highest aspirations at this time. Then, with the completed image in your mind and with your candle alight, cast your paper boat on the water and watch it float away. Thank the angels for their gift of summer bounty and allow the candle to burn out completely.

THE ANGEL OF AUTUMN - ANGEL TARIEL

Autumn is a time for harvest. Now, after all the effort you have put into the garden since Spring, it is time to reap your rewards. Every vegetable, fruit or flower that you enjoy has been touched by angels. Thank Angel Tariel and the devic kingdom for their unswerving support of animal and plant life. Make chutneys and jams with extra fruit and vegetables, and give back as much as possible to the beings of the earth by making a compost of all the growth which has now come to a natural end. Thank the plant life for the gift of itself. Collect leaves and use them as ground cover, which gives food to the insects and earthworms and will also keep away unnecessary weeds.

A Ritual for Autumn Equinox

September 20–23 (Northern Hemisphere);
March 20–23 (Southern Hemisphere)

Wander around your garden and touch the leaves and stems of the flowers and plants. Thank them for sharing themselves with you, for it is the gift of their life force which gives us the energy we need throughout the year. Sit quietly with your eyes closed and imagine yourself as one of those plants or trees. Imagine what it was like for them to produce the sap and the energy to reach up to the sky and down deep into the earth below. Imagine how it is to share your life with insects and birds and other wildlife, and how it feels to

have angels encouraging you to grow. Thank the garden for all its gifts of abundance. Give the plant life around you permission to die down now as we begin to face the end of the growing year.

THE ANGEL OF WINTER - AMABAEL

Amabael is the Angel of Winter, and it's important you don't neglect the garden at this time of the year. Speak to Amabael even when the ground is under several feet of snow. There is lots of life going on down there, even though – like the angels – we can't always see its presence. Imagine Amabael looking after all the life forms under the cold, hard soil or the frozen snow. When you see the sunshine sparkling on an icicle or snowflake, greet Amabael and thank this angel for its comfort and support during this harsh time of year.

As the sun struggles to rise above the horizon on December 21 (or June 21 in the Southern Hemisphere), it's vital that you honour the living things in the world around you. They are all hiding deep down in the protection of the dark earth. You can

encourage the tiny, wintering plants and bulbs to begin to waken up and begin their journey into the brightness again.

A Ritual for the Winter Solstice

December 20–23 (Northern Hemisphere);

June 20–23 (Southern Hemisphere)

The weather and temperature at this time of year doesn't encourage outdoor pursuits, but if possible carry this ritual out in the open simply because you will feel more connected with the earth outside. You will need some cardboard/paper, scissors, four candles and some seeds.

Create a large circle around you either in the soil or else with a string or rope (this symbolizes the Earth). Now cut out a symbol of the Sun and the Moon in cardboard or paper, and place them opposite each other, to the east and to the west, almost touching the circle. (East is where the sun rises in the morning, west is where it sets at night). Stand or sit in the middle of the circle and, within the circle, place one candle at each of the four different directions:

north/south/east/west, and push some seeds into the soil close to the candles. As you light the candles, ask the angel Amatiel and other members of the devic kingdom to come back to the land again and bring new life to the soil.

Close your eyes and imagine the Moon lighting up the earth around you at night-time, then its place is taken by the Sun and feel the warmth of the Sun's rays touching the soil and awakening it. Feel the Sun – know that it is returning to this place again as the weeks unfold. Imagine the Sun warming the earth and encouraging the seeds you've just planted to end their hibernation. Imagine all the growth underground wakening up and beginning to push towards the sunlight. Be that little seedling or bulb in your mind's eye. Unfold from hibernation and begin to seek the light above you. Know that there is a path to follow, there is light at the end of the struggle. Allow your heart to fill with joy as you finally push through to the light! Let the candles burn themselves out.

When to Plant and Tend Your Garden

If you are thinking of planting or specially tending some specific trees, shrubs or flowers, try to do so on the day that is especially powerful for them, as the following chart shows.

THE PLANTING WEEK

Day of the Week	Tree/Shrub/Flower
Sunday	marigold, heliotrope, sunflower, buttercup, cedar, beech, oak
Monday	night flowers, willow, birch, vervain, white rose, white Iris
Tuesday	red rose, pine, daisy, thyme, pepper
Wednesday	fern, lavender, hazel, cherry, periwinkle

Thursday	cinnamon, beech, buttercup, coltsfoot, oak
Friday	pink rose, ivy, birch, heather, clematis, sage, violet, water lily
Saturday	myrrh, moss, coltsfoot, fir

Chapter 5

The Angels of Love

As Paul the apostle said in his First Letter to the Corinthians (1:13.1): 'I may be able to speak the language of men and even of the angels, but if I have no love my speech is no more than a noisy gong or a clanging bell ... Love does not keep a record of wrongs ... Love never gives up. Love is eternal. It is love, therefore, that you should strive for ...'

Sometimes we tend to think of love as merely romance, but it is a lot more than that. Love has a magical energy of its own.

Love can bring miracles, love can change mindsets, and love can even heal the physical body.

Angels are gifts given to us through love. If we don't allow ourselves to love we cannot be open to our angels. We cannot accept love into our life until we have made the effort to show forgiveness to ourselves and to others. Sometimes we fall in love with love when we meet someone we feel is special, but when that person acts in a way we don't appreciate, we can become judgmental and so fall out of love.

True love is unconditional, and this love can be shared with children, with lovers, with colleagues, with strangers and, of course, with angels! We must learn to love ourselves first of all before we can truly love others. By bringing angel magic into your life, you can learn to open up your heart to love, to attract love into your life, and then to commit yourself to love.

I believe we have each chosen to be born into this life to face certain lessons along our journey to spiritual enlightenment. Those lessons can be given many different names and revolve around personal and spiritual development, but on the whole they are lessons on the need for us to learn and practise

unconditional love and forgiveness. No one is perfect, nor are we meant to be. It is because we are imperfect that we need to be present here on Earth so we can heal ourselves of our imperfections, forgiving ourselves and others for being imperfect.

If we lived in the time of Jesus Christ we would use the Aramaic word 'shaw' in place of the word 'forgive'. 'Shaw' means to 'untie', and so by forgiving we untie the bond that holds us to the person we see as the 'transgressor'. Until we learn the lesson of forgiveness we are forever tied to that person and that lesson, and that lesson will come back to us again and again until we pass that test of forgiveness. When someone wrongs us we may feel justified in never wanting to forgive that person – that the 'sinner' does not deserve forgiveness. If we take this attitude, however, we are also stopping good coming to us. We don't tend to realize this, though. The definition of the word 'sin' is a Roman term used in archery meaning 'missing the point', so by not forgiving someone else for 'missing the point' we are stopping ourselves from accepting and receiving the 'supply' of love and abundance we all crave and deserve. Living in unforgiveness will guarantee that we are

in bondage to the person we believe has wronged us, and it is only by being willing to forgive that we break free of that bondage and find freedom.

Think of what happens if you criticize or 'point the finger' at someone. Point a finger right now and look at your hand. You will see that three more fingers are pointing right back at you! That is proof itself that when we judge others we are actually judging ourselves, too.

Take a few moments to think about your own life to date. Who has hurt you? How far back does that hurt go? Has being hurt stopped you from enjoying love today? Have past experiences coloured your opinion of sharing love? Only you can answer these questions with truth.

Forgiveness is the act of consciously allowing ourselves to be free from hurt, anger and pain which we feel another has inflicted on us. No matter who we are or where we are on this Earth, each of us is destined to be hurt by others, sometimes knowingly, at other times, unconsciously. Just pretend for a moment that you can see yourself in silhouette. Because you have been hurt your body is full of dark energy, yet your angels

are around you and they are trying to fill you with a beautiful light pink energy, which is love. How can they do so until you let go of the dark energy of unforgiveness? The price of unforgiveness can be very steep. For when we feel unloved in our life we begin to live in fear. Fear manifests in many ways in our personal lives: in feelings of resentment and criticism, which stops us loving ourselves and others; in a life of confusion and depression, which keeps us living in the dark, and, of course, fear also shows up in our physical bodies as 'dis-ease', which is a symbol of a lack of ease in our lives. The opposite of love is not hate, it is fear. Fear is simply a thought that has grown out of proportion. I read somewhere a little message: 'Fear knocked on the door. Love opened it. No one was there.' When we have the magic of love in our lives we have no room for fear, for 'Those who walk with angels shall learn to soar above the clouds.' Remember, angels are just a call away but they are awaiting our call. We must learn to ask for help before we can expect to receive it. It is only then that the angel magic will begin to work wonders!

It is through understanding and spiritual enlightenment that we learn to forgive. It doesn't happen overnight. We may have

to repeat the steps many times before we feel totally free of that 'tie' of unforgiveness. Think of your mind as a desktop computer. The computer is run by the hard disc which has been programmed with certain types of procedures and methods of action. It can only act on the information with which it has been programmed. If it is to react in a different manner it requires reprogramming and it might take some time before it fully accepts that new information. Sometimes a 'virus' of anger and resentment may try to destroy the newly programmed hard disk, but if we have a 'virus alert' in our heart we can banish it as soon as it shows itself.

Angels are just a call away, but they are awaiting our call.

Rituals for Opening Your Heart to Love

A RITUAL FOR FORGIVING OTHERS

We are all seeking love and it often seems just outside our reach. By learning to forgive others we can move forward and so accept that longed-for love in our life.

1. Before you do anything else, begin by lighting a candle so that you consciously know you are 'in the light'. If you know your angel's name, welcome it by this and know now that you are at least twice as strong as before with your angel by your side. Forgiving someone means you now have to change and the one thing we all fear is change. Allow your angel to help you to welcome that change in your heart by saying the following little 'prayer':

Angel of Love, being of light, please bring enlightenment to me here and now.

Help me to bring magic into my life so that I can share it with others.

Help me to fill my heart with love so that I can share it with others.

Help me to fill my heart with light and love as I speak to you now.

2. Think of the person who appears to be causing a problem in your life at present. Visualize them as you last saw them if possible. Say their name out loud and then say:

   The Light within me salutes the Light within you.

3. Again, think of the person whom you would like to be able to forgive. Say their name out loud and then:

   I forgive you for not being as I wanted you to be, I forgive you and I set you free.

By saying this, you are also setting yourself free from the lesson and hardships of unforgiveness.

A Ritual for Forgiving Yourself

All too often we can 'miss the point' of one of the lessons of life and feel so badly about it that we punish ourselves for years. Instead, we should think of life as a school where we are constantly learning lessons. When we make an error the secret is to learn from it, not repeat it.

We may watch others make mistakes, and notice that they never seem to 'pay' for their actions. Can this be true? No, by the Universal Law of Ten-fold Return (see page xvii) such people will have to repay the debt at some time. Allow time to take its course; try not to judge. What is of greater concern now is freeing yourself of your own tie of bondage. If you are still uneasy about this, keep asking yourself how holding onto the bond of unforgiveness has held you back from sharing and enjoying the love that awaits you. For, imperfect as we may be, God loves us, and our angels love us, so we really should consider loving ourselves. We may have been told that 'loving yourself' is selfish.

This is untrue. It is the first step in learning to love others, and without self-love we cannot have love for others. Despite all those negative, unloving thoughts, those thoughtless actions, we must forgive and love ourselves. Otherwise, how can we follow the instruction 'Love thy neighbour as you love yourself'?

Here is a simple ritual to help you forgive yourself for not being perfect. It is best to do this while you are alone with no distractions. When you realize you have made a mistake, whether today or 20 years ago, look into your eyes in a mirror and say your name aloud, then:

> *I forgive you for not being as I wanted you to be.*
> *I forgive you and I set you free.*

By saying this, you are learning the lesson of forgiveness and loving yourself.

FURTHER RITUALS FOR FORGIVENESS

✦ Whenever you have a shower, or are even washing your hands, you can get into the habit of saying:

The Angels of Love

Transmuting all things negative to all things positive.

This is just another way of saying 'I am washing away any negativity.'

✦ Whether you are waking up, sitting on a bus, stuck in a traffic jam, going to bed ... it doesn't cost anything to say a forgiveness ritual. One of the strongest rituals is to think through your day and all the people you have been in contact with, or even thought about. Ask each one to forgive you if you have thought or said any unkind things about them, and if they have apparently hurt you in any way, forgive them yourself. Forgiveness can be a leap in the dark, and often takes a lot of courage, but when you make a leap in the dark you are guaranteed to come out into the light!

A Ritual for Healing Your Heart

Find some quiet space where you will not be disturbed. Make sure you are comfortable and, as usual, light a candle as a conscious decision to be in the Light, then go within yourself. Ask

your angel to help you at this important time in your life. Now put your hands on your heart and feel once more, and for the last time, the actual heart-felt pain you have been suffering due to the event or the person who has hurt you. Breathe in that pain and bring to mind all the sadness and sense of loss you have held in your heart. Now breathe out all that pain, once and for all. Repeat this exercise as often as you wish until you truly feel that you have cleared your heart of the negative energy.

The next step is to ask your angel to help you find forgiveness in your heart. Try to imagine your angel is sitting in front of you, arms outstretched, just waiting for you to rush into them, end the struggle and accept love.

This ritual can bring up strong emotions, and it's important to realize that crying is a natural remedy for heartfelt sorrow. It creates the hormone serotonin in the bloodstream and thereby helps you to relax and release tension and anxiety.

Imagine your angel is sending you a pink ray of energy straight from its heart to yours. This energy is the energy you need to show love to yourself, and to others. This energy will

now fill up those arid, empty spaces in your heart where love has not been for some time. This energy will help you release through tears the feelings of loss and emptiness you have been holding onto for so long. This energy will lighten up your heart and keep it filled with an ever-increasing supply of love, which will also ensure that this vital organ is in good health.

A Ritual for Healing the Child Within

As a numerologist, I believe we have all been sent here to Earth with a secret blueprint to follow in our Earthly life. Once you crack that blueprint you can make sure that you are doing the right things at the right time along your life path. One very important part of any healing process is to understand that we all have within us what we call 'the Inner Child'.

As we have all come to Earth to learn certain lessons, one of those lessons is given to us between the age of birth to nine years old. Until we heal the hurt from this lesson we never truly develop as adults, as there will always be that one area of our life where we still react like a child. Up until the age of eight to nine years old we are only capable of experiencing life

through our emotions for we haven't yet been taught logic or reasoning. For instance, if your mother went off to hospital without you and returned with a newborn infant, you as a small child would not have understood what was going on with all the demands of an infant baby. Instead, you would probably have felt unloved and abandoned by your mother. You would not be capable of reasoning, 'Mum loves me but she's not able to cuddle me like before because she has a newborn baby who needs feeding.' If you, yourself, had been put into an incubator at birth because your health was in danger, you would not have felt, 'This is the best thing for me if I'm to survive.' No, you would more likely have felt, 'What happened? I've been abandoned! I'm all alone! My mother's left me!' And so if a small child experiences such things, there is a chance that he or she will grow into an adult who has never bonded with their mother, and could therefore also have problems relating to bonding in relationships in later life.

Obviously hundreds of thousands of things happen to each of us within a 12-month period, but there will be something specific in our childhood which had a major impact on each of

us. It doesn't have to be physical or sexual abuse; it can be as simple and ordinary as the examples shown above. But that doesn't take away the pain. Does it have to remain this way? No, it can be healed with rituals such as the following. By the way, you don't have to know exactly what it was that affected your Inner Child, just ask yourself, 'Is there any area in my life where I tend to go over-the-top in my reaction?' (Such as feeling bereft if your lover goes away for a day, or believing there's never any point in speaking about how you feel because no one ever listens.) By recognizing this area, you are now recognizing your 'Inner Child'.

Firstly, though, you have to discover for yourself the age of your own Inner Child, so that you can recall the crisis which you had to face in your childhood. To do this, take the first date of your birthday (the day of the month in which you were born). For instance, if you were born on the 8th of a month this means your Inner Child is 8 years old. If the date of your birthday is a double figure, then add the two numbers together to get a single figure. For example, if you were born on the 23rd of a month you add both numbers together, 2 + 3 (= 5), and this means your Inner Child is 5 years old.

Often people will say to me, 'I can't remember my child-hood.' This is possibly because of the pain felt at that time of crisis, and it would be a natural human reaction to try to block it out along the lines of, 'If I don't think about it then it didn't happen.' Not thinking about the experience, however, doesn't take it away – the hurt is still there. Finding out the age of your Inner Child is the first step towards healing the hurt, even if you cannot consciously remember it.

Visualization Exercise: Healing Your Inner Child

As usual, do the following visualization exercise in a quiet place where you won't be disturbed. If you decide to record the script, speak slowly and gently, and expect the exercise to last about 12–15 minutes. Light a candle, play gentle music in the background and sit in a comfortable place. This exercise is best done when you are by yourself simply so that you can expel your emotions in private if necessary.

Start off by breathing deeply into both lungs, and you may also like to 'root' yourself in the ground during the exercise. Simply imagine tiny magnets are growing from the soles of your feet, and these are keeping you connected to the ground below. Spend as much time as you like becoming relaxed, breathing a colour of your choice into your entire body. The deeper you achieve relaxation, the deeper the healing.

Imagine that you are in a garden or country place and you are watching the following scenario going on. (If you find it difficult to be visual, perhaps you can pretend to yourself that you are watching this as though it is a programme on TV.) An angel is walking down the garden path. There are trees and bushes around the pathway but the angel seems to know exactly the direction to take. As you watch, you notice it is nearing sunset and perhaps you can even see the bright Sun setting and feel the warm, gentle rays of the Sun touching your skin. You feel relaxed and calm as the scenario unfolds.

Now you hear a small child crying. As the angel continues along the path the cries become louder. They are heart-wrenching

sobs and you realize the angel immediately wants to find this child and do what it can to console it.

You see the angel walk off the path and walk under the trees. Now the angel finds the little child who is crying. The angel picks up the child and sits it gently on its knee. As the child continues to cry the angel calmly offers love and consolation. 'What can I do to help?' the child is asked. 'Why are you so upset?' Now you realize that this little child is you, yourself. Know that you are safe and secure and the one being in your life who never judges you is here right now. Perhaps amid sobs or with just a gentle understanding you now discover what the problem has been.

Now you watch as the angel explains to the little child exactly what happened and why it happened, and helps this little child to understand and so heal the feeling of abandonment and fear that has caused such grief. The angel gently enfolds the little child in love amid assurances that it is here to love and guard her or him forever. Now the two of you have some fun together and you can hear the little child laughing with joy.

This is the first step towards healing your Inner Child. Emotions don't always heal overnight, so be patient as it can take time. As you are healing your Inner Child, be kind to yourself. Treat yourself as though you are a little child going through a trauma. Be gentle with yourself and don't expect too much. After all, if you broke a leg you wouldn't expect to be out of the plastercast immediately, and you would get a lot of sympathy from those around you in the meantime! Soon you will notice that angel magic will begin to show up in tiny ways in your life.

THE POWER OF ANGEL LOVE

Love is a vibrant energy and not just a romantic emotion. Until we open up our own heart to love for ourselves we cannot ever accept and enjoy true love – another word for unconditional love – from anyone else. You can be a magical magnet for love, however, when you open up to your angel's pure loving energy.

When you have enjoyed the following ritual, watch out for small changes in all your relationships from now on. Some may

work like magic; some may take more time. However, once you have done this visualization exercise nothing can remain the same!

Next time you meet someone with whom you may have had a disagreement, act as though you have amnesia about the last time you encountered each other and begin completely afresh. You don't have to become bosom-buddies, but showing forgiveness and compassion to others works magic in our own lives.

Visualization Exercise:
A Ritual for Opening Your Heart to Angel Love

By now you should be used to finding a quiet place to enjoy these visualizations where you will not be disturbed. If you are doing this visualization alone, take time recording the script, which should last 30–35 minutes. (Remember you can change the word 'you' to 'I' if you wish.) Otherwise, if you are in a group, have someone read the script out. And don't forget the importance of regular deep breathing in order to help you let go of any tension and relax into this visualization exercise.

Once you are in a comfortable sitting position, begin to breathe in slowly and rhythmically. Listen to your inward and outward breath. Now imagine tiny magnets are on the soles of your feet and these are keeping you connected to the Earth below. This will keep you grounded during your journey. Now imagine you are breathing into every cell of your body. Feel the pores of your skin gently open to increase the depth of your breathing. You are now able to feel yourself breathing directly into your central core. The deeper the breath, the more relaxed you become. It is lovely and peaceful, and you know that your body is benefiting from this exercise. How easy it is becoming to relax and visualize. You welcome these moments.

As you go deeper within, you begin to remember the past. Go back in years and remember all the people you have loved. Remember the pain in your heart when you felt they no longer loved you. What did it feel like? Did it leave a dark space in your heart? Are there scars in your heart now like huge holes or fissures? Are they small cracks which are difficult to close? What do you need to heal these scars? Invite your angel into your

heart. Your angel brings you whatever you need. It helps to heal the scars. Now the scars are being healed. The darkness is leaving your heart. Your heart is no longer heavy. The burden of pain is leaving your heart. Rest for a while as your heart is being healed.

Now remember the joy of being loved and of loving. Remember how your heart lifted when you shared time with someone you cared for and who cared for you. Remember the wonderful feeling when you shared love from your heart with someone else.

Now I want you to imagine that your angel is in front of you. You may feel it, you may see it, or you may just sense it. You know your angel wants to share its love with you; it doesn't want you to feel separated or isolated anymore. Feel yourself holding out your arms to your angel. You feel no fear – you feel only love. Allow your tears to flow if this is right for you, for they will become tears of joy. Now sense your angel is hugging you. You know with absolute certainty that your heart is now open to angel love.

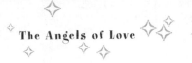

Imagine that you see a ray of golden light coming from your angel's heart and beaming into your own. A door opens in your heart to receive this golden love. Each time you breathe in, the golden light of your angel's love enters your heart, and each time you breathe out, any fear or tension leaves it. And as you breathe in again, your heart is once more filled with love, and as you breathe out, any tension or negativity leaves it. And as you breathe in, your angel's love heals any scars of hurt or pain in your heart, and as you breathe out, you release any pain, now and forever. And as you breathe in, your angel's love lights up any dark areas in your heart and as you breathe out, you release any darkness now and forever.

You continue to breathe in your angel's love until it feels as though your heart is completely filled with this golden light of love. And now you know you have so much love you can actually share it with your angel. So now, as you breathe out, an arc of golden light moves out from your heart and into your angel's heart. And as you breathe in your angel's love, you breathe out love to your angel. And now you see there is a circle of love

moving between you and your angel. How wonderfully full of love you feel. And you know that you will never forget this moment. You have never felt such lightness, such joy or such love.

You realize there is so much love here that you would like to share it. You feel light and carefree, completely buoyed up by the lightness of your angel's love. You know you can leave this place now, quite safely, and fly with your angel to any place in your world which needs love right now. It's easy. Allow yourself to lift off the ground gently and fly with your angel. Your angel is help-ing you, supporting you. You know you are safe. You know you are loved. Now that you've left all the weight of negative living behind and you are free and light and filled with the golden light of angel love.

Now you want to visit some place in your life which feels a lack of love. Perhaps it's your home, your family or your place of work. You can go to all these places. It's easy to bring the magic of angel love to these places. Just imagine you are there and you will be. As you approach, these places seem grey and drab because there is no love there. But now as you fly over these

places with your angel you see a great change taking place. It's as though it's raining love. The energy of angel love is lighting up these places and the people who are there. Look down and see what happens when the light reaches them. Invite those people out of their greyness, into the light of love. See how the entire environment changes when it is touched by angel love. The light of angel love has transformed the negativity into joy. Watch the magical effect!

Now it's time to leave and return to where you began this journey. But know that you can come back here whenever you wish to enjoy sharing the magic of love between yourself and your angel.

And now I want you to take a deep breath and, as you breathe in and out again, you can once more feel the ground beneath your feet. And now, as you breathe in and out again, you can once more feel your fingertips and your toes. And now, as you breathe in and out, it's time to open your eyes, and you do so, coming back into this room, feeling relaxed, refreshed and much more loved than ever before.

Rituals for Attracting Love

Once you have freed yourself from judgement and unforgiveness, it's time to bring more joy and fun into your life. There are lots of enjoyable rituals you can practise so that you attract more love into your life. Love comes in all guises: supportive family, generous friendships, harmonious relationships and, of course, romance!

Always remember, however, you cannot force anyone to love you, and that love must first begin within yourself before you can seek sincere love outside.

+ If you want to attract a particular person into your life, ask the angels to be with you when you meet. Remember the other party also has at least one angel, so speak to your own angel and say how you feel. It is possible for the two angels to get together and communicate about your love. Don't be too demanding, though, for sometimes a person or relationship may not be right for you at that moment, for instance the timing may be wrong or the current lesson you are

learning may require you to be alone for the moment. Rather than becoming fixated on getting the love you want, just ask your angel for 'the perfect outcome' in the situation. Then accept whatever happens as 'the perfect outcome'.

Whether you are seeking romance, forgiveness, healing a misunderstanding, or simply a telephone call from a particular person, one way to ensure that the 'perfect outcome' happens is to write a letter to the other person's angel, just as you would to a human being! It's simple, begin with *'Dear Angel of ___ (name),'* and state what you want help with. Always remember there are two sides to everything, so again ask for *'the perfect outcome between me and ___'*. Let's say you met a man named John, but never got around to exchanging phone numbers. In this case you could write: *'Dear Angel of John, Please help John find some way of contacting me with the perfect outcome for both of us.'* Note, you don't insist that John phones you, you just ask his angel to help him find a way of contacting you, then it's up to John to follow through!

✦ Now that you have opened up your heart to love, begin to show love to your body by eating sensibly. The only eating regimen you need is a Diet of Love. Every time you are tempted to criticize yourself or to eat or drink too much, simply say your name, then 'I love you.' When you get used to saying this you won't need to compensate yourself for any lack of love because you will now be filling yourself with it!

✦ Use some of the gifts of Mother Earth and invite the Angels of Love, archangel Gabriel, archangel Uriel and, of course, Cupid, to join you as you blend some aromatherapy oils to attract love into your life. Bear in mind that choosing to work on the day that is powerful for each of the angels of love can also help: Gabriel's day is Monday (which celebrates the Moon, and you know how romantic moonlight is!), while Uriel's days are Tuesday (or Mardi, named after Mars, the sign of male sexuality) and Friday (also Vendredi, named after Venus!).

Here is how you make a sexy blend to attract love. Get a small dark-coloured bottle and pour a carrier oil, such as

almond, olive or grapeseed oil, into the bottle. Then add to the bottle the following:

3 drops of rose or rosewood essential oil

3 drops of sandalwood essential oil

3 drops of ylang ylang or jasmine essential oil

Shake the bottle gently then dab some oil on your wrists and behind your ears, and on other pulse points if you wish.

Essential oils can also be used in an oil burner. Generally, the burner will have a reservoir in which you place first water and then a few drops of your chosen oil or oils. To help attract love into your life, add drops of the following oils to the water:

2 drops of patchouli essential oil

2 drops of orange or neroli essential oil

2 drops of cinnamon essential oil

✦ Attract the angels of love to be with you by wearing necklaces of rose quartz crystal. Other crystals that attract love are aventurine and citrine. There are many different designs of angel pins now available. Try to find one which has rose quartz, aventurine or citrine.

Wearing the colours red (for passion), pink (for self-esteem and unconditional love) and peach/apricot (for emotional flow) can also help attract the right energies to you.

✦ Light a special candle to draw love to you and ensure it burns out all the way. The candle can be green (for heart energy), pink (for love) or red (for passion). If you have someone special in mind already, and if you have anything belonging to them, then place an angel figurine on top of, or close by, this object.

✦ If you are planning a romantic liaison, before the arrival of your guest burn incense sticks such as jasmine, rose, patchouli or neroli. Choose a tablecloth and candle in red or pink and place a vase of honeysuckle, violets or roses on the table. There's nothing like a sensually scented room lit by the glow of candlelight to encourage romance and passion!

Rituals for Committing Yourself to Love

THE ANGELS OF THE FOUR DIRECTIONS RITUAL

The angels know what you want (they are angels, after all!), but often we need to commit ourselves consciously by enacting a certain ritual. This involves connecting with the Angels of the Four Directions: North, South, East and West. (If you don't know which direction is which, ask yourself where does the Sun rise in the morning? That's east – and where it sets at the end of the day is west. If you stand with the west to your left and the east to your right, then the direction in front of you is north, and the direction behind you is south.) If you are seeking a new love in your life you will need some **crushed cardamom seeds**, but if you want to attract someone back into your life get hold of some **rosemary herb**. As I mentioned in Chapter 1, the four archangels, Michael, Raphael, Uriel and Gabriel, look after the four compass directions.

Carry out this ritual outside if at all possible. Stand facing the north and, blowing just a fraction of the cardamom seed (or rosemary) towards the north, say:

Archangel Michael, Angel of the North, please take with you to the northern direction my request to bring me success in this venture.

Now stand facing east, and blowing just a fraction of the cardamom seed (or rosemary) towards the east, say:

Archangel Uriel, Angel of the East,
please take with you to the easterly direction my
request to bring success in this venture.

Next, stand facing south, and blowing just a fraction of the cardamom seed (or rosemary) towards the south, say:

Archangel Raphael, Angel of the South,
please take with you to the southerly direction my
request to bring success in this venture.

Finally face west, and blowing just a fraction of the cardamom seed (or rosemary) towards the west, say:

The Angels of Love

Archangel Gabriel, Angel of the West,
please take with you to the westerly direction my
request to bring success in this venture.

Once you have completed this task, thank the angels for their help and understand that there is no need to repeat it.

THE 5-STEPS RITUAL FOR A LOVING PARTNER

Without realizing it, sometimes we tend to be unfocused in our desires. We know we want something different than what we have, but we may not be completely committed to attaining it. It is as though we go into a travel agents and say, 'I want to book a flight,' and when the salesperson asks us 'Where to?' we shrug and say 'I just want to book a flight.' How can we expect to arrive at our goals until we decide what they are? With the angels' help we can use 'The 5-Steps Ritual' to ensure we fulfil our aspirations. This ritual requires you to write things down, so you will need a pen, paper (pink, the colour of love, if possible) and an envelope.

First of all, think carefully about what you wish to achieve – a permanent relationship, a short-term romance – be sure you want what you ask for! Try not to be too precise in describing a person because this can be limiting. For instance, you might ask for someone who is 6 ft in height with blue eyes. Now the person who the angels want you to meet could be 5 ft 10 in with green eyes! Also, you may usually be interested in someone who is in a profession, while the perfect person for you could be in a trade. Just so you don't shoot yourself in the foot by describing someone who isn't for you, simply state *'the perfect partner for me right now'*. Make sure you follow the full five steps. Once you have carried out this ritual, know that it will be put into motion for you at the time that is right for you, and that could be one day or one year from today's date. Once it is in the hands of the angels you can sit back and trust them to know when the time is perfect for you.

Here is how you do 'The 5-Steps Ritual'. Write down the following, choosing the words that seem right for you:

Dear Archangel Gabriel (or Uriel),

I, ___ [your name], make a conscious decision to meet the perfect partner/companion/lover right now.

I commit myself to meeting the perfect partner/companion/lover right now.

I affirm that I have now met the perfect partner/companion/lover right now.

Thank you, archangel Gabriel (or Uriel), for helping me to meet the perfect partner/companion/lover right now.

I now let go and leave this request in the hands of the angels.

Then sign your full name and put the date on the letter.

You will notice from the above that all those statements are in the present tense. That is because Universal Law (and that includes the angels) live in the present. (Universal Law is a fact of physics which we have no power over, such as 'what you give out comes back to you with more force.') If you wrote a statement in the future, such as *'I will meet ...'*, that is stating something that can happen tomorrow and, as you know, tomorrow never comes! Looking back over those five steps, you will see that you make a **conscious decision**, you **commit** yourself to that action, you **affirm** it is the truth, and you **thank the angels** for giving it to you. By signing and dating it you are now fulfilling your obligation to have this come into your life. Put the letter into the envelope, then place under an angel figurine or picture if you have one and **'let go'** of your request, knowing it is being looked after by the angels.

Chapter 6

The Angels of Divine Abundance

Abundance comes in all shapes and sizes, not in financial wealth alone, but the most obvious way of assessing wealth is by looking at our bank account or our possessions, such as house, car, clothes, holiday destinations ... the list goes on! It is imperative to realize that our own self-worth will ultimately affect our financial worth, yet often we can get that fact (and it is a fact) turned the other way round – that our self-worth is based on our financial worth. Then there can be the belief that there is something wrong with being wealthy, and both of these

beliefs are usually held by those of us who were brought up in straitened circumstances. Because of the way we heard money described, such as 'filthy lucre', 'dirty money', 'money is the root of all evil', 'money doesn't grow on trees', we can get some very odd ideas about what it portrays in our life. I certainly did! Yet most of our ideas are incorrect. Money is just money. It is what each of us does with money that brings about the outcome: whether it has a positive or negative influence. It's not money's fault if half the world is abundant and the other half is starving. It's not money's fault if millions are spent to buy a prized painting while that same amount could be used to vaccinate thousands of children from cholera or typhoid and so save lives. Money is just money. It is what each of us uses it for that has the result to feed either need or greed. The belief that 'Money is the root of all evil' is a misquote. The correct statement is 'The love of money above all else is the root of all evil.' And as for 'Money doesn't grow on trees' it does, you know, if you are a forester, or own orchards!

I come from a background of 'poverty consciousness' as we call it now. This is not to criticize my parents or family, just to state a fact. When I was just a baby I became very ill and, as no one could discover the problem, I was taken to many hospitals around Ireland and I was separated from my family for several weeks. When the medics finally cured the problem my mother came to collect me from the hospital. This was over 20 miles away from our home, and as we didn't own a car she'd had to hire a car and driver for the day, which was an enormous expense. When I was handed to her she was overjoyed that I was in her arms again, healthy once more. Then ... nightmare! She was presented with a bill for £32 and expected to pay it there and then. Needless to say, she didn't have anything like that amount on her (this was way before the days of credit cards!) and horror of horrors, I was taken out of her arms and was not going to be given back until the bill was paid. Naturally my mother was devastated, so much so that the hospital relented, but the dreadful fear of being separated from some-one I loved and who loved me was deeply impressed into me from that moment. And what was its cause? Lack of money! Eight years later my family and I emigrated to Britain and that move was also precipitated due to our straitened circumstances.

The change from one environment and culture to another brought me into years of confusion and isolation and what did I believe caused it ... the lack of money! And so, year after year I equated lack of money with confusion, dread, fear, isolation, dispossession, and any other word you can think of that describes a living nightmare.

I let myself believe that money had power while I had no power, so it got out of proportion in my life. When, many years later, I began my path of healing, I went through a nightmare few years when I had a tiny hand-to-mouth income, with the responsibility of a mortgage and a car loan, and all the extra expenses these bring with them. I spent most of those times 'robbing Peter to pay Paul' with overdrafts which got bigger and bigger and the help of my credit cards. With hindsight, I realized that I had had to face all these problems because I had not at that time healed my 'Inner Child' (see Chapter 5). In those days I literally used to wake up in the middle of the night having nightmares that the house or the car had been repossessed! The bank must have noticed my precarious position but they never harassed me. It wasn't till I had sorted myself out

that I realized why. While I had been blind to it, they had seen that I was a person of worth, or at least they had assessed my home as a property of worth! They knew I was living in a gold-mine, though I had my vision totally blinkered by my fear of the lack of money in my life.

So, how did I turn it all around? With the help of my angels, of course! And just in case you think that angels wouldn't bother with matters such as money, both archangel Gabriel and the angel Parasiel are the angels of abundance and that, as you know, includes money! Angels, like God, work in mysterious and magical ways.

I remember getting a phone call several years ago from a young man who was pretty suicidal. He had heard me talking on the radio about angels and was desperately seeking a meeting with me. He lived some miles away and had no transport except public bus, but he didn't have enough money to come into town to meet me, even though I wasn't going to charge anything for a reading. I remember saying to him, 'If you're meant to come and meet me the angels will make sure you will' and put the situation in the hands of the angels. The next day

he rang me, ecstatic. He had put the bins out the night before and there, on the ground in his back yard, was a £10 note. It was clean, unused and crisp to the touch, despite the fact that it had been raining only moments before he found it. Needless to say, he came in for the reading!

Similar situations have happened to me several times. I remember especially one experience which happened when I was feeling rather down in the mouth because I had no cash. I was doing my laundry and had just put the newly-washed clothes onto the top of the washing machine when the phone rang. It was someone looking for help and, of course, I gave it. After the call I was thinking 'I'm mad doing all these things for free', and I went to take the washed clothes outside. On the top of the washing I found a clean £5 note. The note was new but just slightly damp from the wet clothes. I thanked the angels for that, knowing that they were repaying me for giving my time freely on the phone to someone in need. I have also received other sums of money and crystals, all from my angels within my home.

Before trying any magic with your angel regarding abundance, firstly it is important to understand how you actually

feel about money. As always, the angels cannot force you to do anything – the decision that you will accept more goodness into your life is up to you! They cannot and will not force you to become abundant! And that does include allowing yourself to accept all the good and abundance that is there for you. If you even feel a twinge of embarrassment or guilt reading this chapter, this suggests you may need to heal your attitude towards money.

The following are some simple exercises you can carry out to find out just how you feel about money.

How Do You Feel About Money?

1. Finish this sentence out loud: 'Money is ...'
2. Now write out ten sentences about money, each time finishing the statement 'Money is ...' Keep going till you have made up the full ten sentences. It's amazing how difficult it may seem if you do find you have a problem accepting financial support in your life.

3. Close your eyes and imagine that you are entering a bank that is familiar to you. Now a bank official is taking you through some locked doors into the area where special deposits are kept in boxes. The room is full from floor to ceiling with these boxes. You know they hold some special contents. The official hands you a key which you know will open the box belonging to you. Perhaps you see names on some of the boxes as you glance around, and then you find your own. It has your name clearly marked on it and you open it with the key in your hand. Now look inside and see what it contains. This is yours and yours alone.

What did you find in the special deposit box: old newspaper, gold bullion, bills owed, fake jewellery? Was it full to the brim with currency and cheques, or was it empty?

It may be difficult to understand or accept this, but what you said, what you wrote and what you saw in each of the above exercises is symbolic of how you view money in your

own life. Ask yourself what do the symbols mean? Where did you get those ideas about money?

Ask yourself what would happen if you didn't have a money 'problem', if you had no pressing bills coming through the letterbox? If you won the lottery and paid everything off, what would you do? How would it change your life? Be absolutely honest with yourself when you answer this. Perhaps when you really look at the reason for staying in financial penury you may find it is just a pattern you learned as a child (such as 'There's never enough to go around' / 'In one door, out the other').

What would happen if you were financially successful, what would change? Is change what frightens you? Or is penury the sticking plaster that ensures you stay in an unfulfilling relationship rather than break free and start over? Perhaps what you need is courage, rather than cash! Again, our self-worth is what guarantees our financial worth. Through accepting love and support from your angels through the following rituals you can begin to fill yourself with a healthy self-esteem.

The angels cannot force you to do anything – the decision to accept more abundance into your life is up to you!

Rituals for Drawing Divine Abundance to You

As Thursday is governed by Jupiter, the planet of expansion, this is the best day to look for abundance in any area of your life. Wear purple, yellow, green or gold. These colours draw abundance towards you. The same colours can be used in candles to bring 'enlightenment' to the financial situation.

I mentioned earlier that there is a universal law called 'The Universal Law of Ten-fold Return' (see page xvii), guaranteeing that what you give out comes back to you ten times greater. Here are several rituals you can practise which puts this universal law into practice:

A Ritual For Changing your mind

Our words – whether spoken or merely thought – create the world in which we live. I never realized this so clearly until I

156

actually 'thought' myself into poverty. Well, when you hit rock-bottom there is only one way to go, and it had to start with my words changing. Instead of thinking 'I won't have enough' when I found myself at the cashier's in a supermarket, I began to think the word 'wealth'. I didn't say 'I have more than enough money' because I knew I didn't, and I was aware of all those bills at home! By saying the word 'wealth', however, I began to change my thinking pattern and as I was 'giving out' wealth, it had to come back to me, according to the Universal Law of Ten-fold Return. And it did! Nowadays, if ever I feel shaky in any areas I simply say or think 'Health, Wealth and Wisdom, thank you, angels!' That covers just about anything and everything!

A very simple way of bringing abundance to you is to simply say: *'The Angel of Divine Abundance goes before me and prepares my way.'* It's especially helpful if you need to ask for extra credit from a financial institution. Archangel Gabriel and angel Parasiel are the two angels looking after our financial worth. Choose a picture of an angel, or an angel figurine, and place it on top of any bills you have which may be causing you a problem. Any time you think of 'How will I pay this?'

immediately follow on with the words *'The Angel of Divine Abundance is doing perfect work through me right now.'* You will be amazed at how things are worked out. In fact, this ritual pretty much sorts all your financial affairs out, if you let it!

Remember we are what we think we are, so you must allow the angel magic of abundance to come into your life. There is no point in your angels trying to heap abundance on you at every given moment if you keep turning away from it. One of the 'inspirations' my angels sent me was 'Prepare for a miracle'. I thought about those words for some time and then I realized why they had said 'prepare' rather than 'There's a miracle coming up'. It was because I was so downcast about myself I would easily have walked straight by any financial reward that came 'out of the blue'. I would have been certain it was waiting there for someone else so I needed to 'prepare' myself to accept the goodness that was there for me. Do you need to 'prepare' to accept good things? If so, begin now by changing your words and your thoughts with the help of the Angel of Divine Abundance.

A Ritual for Tithing

When every penny you make seems to go straight out again, it's easy to believe that you never, ever make any money. I certainly believed that until I got into the habit of following a simple tithing ritual which proved quite the opposite. (Tithing – putting one-tenth aside – is an ancient ritual used all around the world and is the original idea of paying a tax whether in money or in goods.) It's simple. All you need do is take one-tenth of your take-home income and set it aside in a separate savings account or a moneybox. (If you are doing this at home put an angel figure – preferably coloured gold – close to the moneybox.) One-tenth of £100 is very little – in fact it's £10. One-tenth of £25 is £2.50. At the time when I began this ritual I was charging £25 for a psychic reading, and it seemed almost a waste of time to put £2.50 into my moneybox after each reading. However, I did get into the habit of doing so and, after a month, would open up the box and add up what I had saved. Whatever the amount was I would then multiply it by ten and that would prove to me what my actual income was. So if I had saved £30 in a month it would show I had made £300, and if I

had saved £75 it would prove I had made ten times that, £750. Before long I began to realize that I did, indeed, have an income (even though most of it was going out to pay bills) and that helped me to change my mind about my ability to bring abundance into my life.

Now there is a very important rule about the money you save through tithing in this way: you have to spend the money on yourself, it must not go to anyone else! When you are happy with spending money on yourself (which can be quite difficult when you are out of the habit of treating yourself well), you can then begin to spend it on other things and other people.

So when you have proven that you do have an income by tithing to yourself, and when you have spent some months treating yourself with these savings, you might then feel there is enough abundance in your life to share it with others. There are many churches which welcome tithes, but if you don't feel close to one perhaps instead you could tithe to a charity of your choice or even to a start-up business project to help someone else (in the latter case it is called 'seed money'). Do it with an open heart, but if you ever feel insecure about this, just remind

yourself of the Universal Law of Ten-fold Return and the Angel of Divine Abundance. With both on your side it has to come back to you no matter what the odds!

A RITUAL FOR USING AFFIRMATIONS

Affirmations are simple, positive statements that, when used on a regular basis, help to alter your beliefs, habits and expectations from those which may be less conducive to those which are much more so. As I explained earlier, I didn't complicate my mind by saying long, involved affirmations to bring abundance into my life. I just kept it simple by saying the single word 'wealth'. As you feel more secure in your credibility make up ten positive affirmations about money and write them out. Be aware of the power of each word, and keep each affirmation in the present tense. There is no point in saying 'Tomorrow I'll be wealthy' because tomorrow never comes! You may like to start off with something like the following: 'I'm rich and I'm proud of it!' or 'I'm so rich I can share!' Now say each affirmation out loud at least seven times. Always be aware of the words you use. Say the all-encompassing 'everything' rather than the

limiting 'anything'. Say 'more than enough' rather than 'enough'. And always remember the Angel of Divine Abundance is close by to help you out.

THE 5-STEPS RITUAL TO ABUNDANCE

As I explained earlier, when you commit your ideas and beliefs to the written word you are giving them even more power. With the angels' help we can use 'The 5-Steps Ritual' once more to help us accept financial abundance. This is similar to the ritual for a loving partner, but this time see if you can get tinted paper (either green, purple or one that has some gold on it), a pen that writes with gold ink, or a narrow paintbrush and gold ink, and an envelope. (If you cannot get gold ink, use a green or purple felt-tip pen.) Finally, all you have to do is decide how much money you wish to have.

Now follow these five steps:

The Angels of Divine Abundance

Dear archangel Gabriel (or Parasiel),

I, ___ (your name), make a conscious decision to accept £___ or more into my life right now.

I commit myself to accepting £ ___ or more into my life right now.

I affirm that I now have £___ or more in my life right now.

Thank you, archangel Gabriel (or Parasiel), for helping me attain £___ or more in my life right now.

I now let go and leave this request in the hands of the angels.

Now sign your full name and put the date on the letter. Place the letter in the envelope, put an angel picture or figurine sitting on it or close by it, and let the angels do the rest for you.

The main thing is to leave it up to them at this point. Don't interfere – just accept with gratitude.

A RITUAL USING MONEY SYMBOLS

Isn't it interesting how we often overlook the obvious when we are going through difficult times? One simple little ritual which you can carry out once a month, or whenever you feel the need, is to use the gifts from nature to help your bank balance along. Just put a dab of bergamot oil or peppermint oil on your bankbook, cheque book, post office savings book, and so on, and you will soon notice how the money seems to multiply rather than disappear. After all, money comes from a 'mint', doesn't it!

There are little bags of 'angel confetti' available in the shops nowadays and if you place one or two of these little angel symbols in your bankbooks and your purse, you will find that financial worry flies out the window if you let it.

Crystals can also act like magnets to draw money to you. Carry a small citrine stone in your purse and you will soon find it is never empty. A citrine 'tumble stone' should cost less

than £1 ($1.60). If you can't find citrine, choose any gold-coloured stone.

A Ritual For Asking for a Loan

When you ask for a loan you are asking for 'credibility'. Thursday is the best day to look for financial abundance (because it is governed by Jupiter, the planet of expansion). Wear something of a gold colour to attract gold into your life.

Before you go into your meeting, ask the angel Parasiel to be with you as you walk through the door. Say:

Glorious angel Parasiel, come with me as I approach this person. Be in front of me. Be behind me. Be to the right of me. Be to the left of me. Please shine your light on my credibility this day.

And remember to say thanks!

The Angels of the Four Directions Ritual

A similar ritual to the one mentioned in Chapter 5 can be used to bring money into your life by asking help from the Angels of

the Four Directions: North, South, East and West. In this case, you need to have some **powdered peppermint** to throw to the four winds. Use dried herbs of pennyroyal or spearmint if you wish, or if you are stuck literally crush a peppermint sweet. Carry out this ritual outside if at all possible. Stand facing the north and, blowing just a fraction of the mint towards the north, say:

Archangel Michael, Angel of the North, please take with you to the northern direction my request to bring me success in this venture.

Now stand facing east, and blowing just a fraction of the mint towards the east, say:

Archangel Uriel, Angel of the East, please take with you to the easterly direction my request to bring success in this venture.

Now stand facing south, and blowing just a fraction of the mint towards the south, say:

Archangel Raphael, Angel of the South, please take with you to the southerly direction my request to bring success in this venture.

Finally, stand facing west, and blowing just a fraction of the mint towards the west, say:

Archangel Gabriel, Angel of the West, please take with you to the westerly direction my request to bring success in this venture.

When you have completed this task, thank the angels for their help and understand that there is no need to repeat it.

Visualization Exercise: The Orchard of Abundance Ritual

If you want to record this visualization exercise, make sure you speak slowly with lots of pauses between sentences so that you can fully relax when you are playing it back. This exercise should take about 20–25 minutes in total. As always it is important that you are in a comfortable sitting position when you do this visualization and that you will not be disturbed – so unplug the phone and turn off the mobile!

Always begin such an exercise by connecting yourself with the Earth. That is simply imagining yourself with tiny little roots or magnets coming from the soles of your feet and connecting into the Earth below.

When you have done this, simply close your eyes and continue to breathe deeply for a few moments. Try to imagine, as you breathe in, that you are standing under a waterfall that showers down golden water on your head. It is soothing and supportive as it touches your hair, and then you breathe it in and it moves down in your forehead, then into your eyes, cheekbones, nose and ears. Now the golden liquid covers your mouth and your scalp, and then moves down your neck as you breathe it in. It is a wonderful feeling being showered with gold. You can sense the angels are laughing joyfully because you have now opened up to receiving their abundance. Now the golden liquid moves over your shoulders and down into your arms. It fills your elbows and moves down your lower arms and into your hands, fingers and thumbs.

As you continue to gently breathe in the golden liquid, it now moves down over your chest, down your back and all the way down your spine. As it moves down the vertebrae of your spine it is as though it is moving down a staircase, step by step, gently and easily. Now the golden liquid moves into your heart and your lungs, and moves down to your waist. It is a wonderful feeling being filled up with golden energy.

And as you breathe in, the golden liquid now moves into your stomach, into the lower torso, helping you to digest life with ease and joy. Now it moves into your organs of elimination and into your hips. The gentle golden liquid helps you to move forward without being tied to the past.

Now the liquid moves down your legs and into your thighs. You feel relaxed, warm and comfortable. You know the loving abundance of your angels is healing you now. You enjoy the feeling as the golden liquid moves into your knees, your calves, your shins and down into your ankles. Now it is moving across your feet into your toes, and all the while your body is filled with the wonderful golden energy of the golden waterfall. You welcome

this golden energy into your life and thank the angels for their help and generosity.

Now imagine that you are outside a walled garden. There is a doorway in front of you. You open the door and, as you step inside, you know that your angel has joined you here today.

You find yourself in a large walled garden. There are many trees in the garden, and you realize it is an orchard. You see lots of people about, and you know that their angel is with them. Your own angel greets you and beckons you to follow a particular path. You do so. The pathway passes many people who are busy collecting their harvest from their trees. Your angel explains that everyone has their own tree, and now you know you are making your way to your own.

You feel quite excited. You never knew you had your own tree before and you wonder what awaits you. Now you see that in the near distance a particular tree seems to stand out. Its branches are laden with all sorts of strange fruits. As you come closer, you realize the branches aren't carrying fruits, they are carrying money! Your angel explains that this is your special tree. All the harvest is for you and you alone. You see there is a huge harvest awaiting you.

Looking around you find a receptacle which you can use to carry away your harvest. Your angel reaches up to a nearby branch of your tree and shows you how to shake it. You do so. The branch feels heavy as you shake it and now money starts falling down around you. It is as though you are standing under the waterfall again, being showered with abundance! You notice all sorts of denominations of notes and some cheques with your name as the receiver. You might even recognize some of the signatures on the cheques. You begin to collect your harvest in the receptacle you chose. Soon it is filled with abundance, yet there is plenty more still on the tree.

Your angel reminds you that this is your tree and you can come back and shake one of its branches whenever you feel you need extra abundance in your life. You feel light and cheerful as you carry your abundance back with you. You know there will be more than enough left on the tree no matter how often you visit this Orchard of Abundance.

You thank your angel for its generosity and for being your companion here today. Now, you open the door of the walled garden and feel yourself sitting here once more. You take a deep breath in and now, as you breathe out, you can feel your fingers and your toes. As you breathe in and out again, now you can feel your entire body from the top of your head to the soles of your feet. And now, as you breathe in and out again, you know it is time for you to open your eyes and return to this room, feeling refreshed and much more abundant than before.

What sort of receptacle did you choose to use? Some people choose a teacup, others a huge wicker basket. Whatever you chose is right for you at the moment, but do remember that with your special Orchard of Abundance you can return to it as often as you like and there is more than enough for everyone there.

I have used this visualization for some years and it never fails to work. Often I just imagine I am standing beneath my Tree of Abundance and simply shake a branch and I know money will come tumbling into my life in the very near future.

Chapter 7
The Angels of Protection

At school you may have learned about guardian angels and how to pray to them by saying:

Oh Angel of God, my guardian dear,
To whom God's love commits me here,
Ever this day/night be at my side,
To light and guard, to rule and guide.

And there was also:

Angel Magic

Matthew, Mark, Luke and John,
Bless the bed that I lay on.
Four corners to my bed,
Four angels 'round me spread:
One at the head, one at the feet
And two to guard me while I sleep ...

These simple words have offered safety and consolation to many a young child over the years. Isn't it a shame that as adults we tend to forget to talk to angels and ask for their protection? I know I have often forgotten, and instead have spent many hours and even days going around in a panic with questions whirling around in my head keeping me distracted rather than intuitive, until finally I am nudged to get help from the higher energies of angels. All we have to do is ask them for help, but maybe it can seem 'too simple to work', so we don't even give it a try. What a waste of our time and energy. Thank heavens the angels seem to have a never-ending source of patience and understanding!

The Angels of Protection

There are countless stories of how angels have magically appeared in people's lives when they are facing a crisis or life-threatening danger. All over the world such stories have been recorded over the decades, and it seems that we are hearing them more and more in the last few years. Many television stations have produced documentaries on such occurrences, and there are numerous books covering this theme. In most instances these arresting beings seem to appear 'out of the blue' and leave just as quickly after effecting an act of protection.

Historically, the archangel Michael is the Angel of Protection and he is often depicted holding a sword as a symbol of his purpose. He is here to defend the weak and protect those who are facing dangers of any sort. Pictorially he is shown slaying a dragon, the symbol of the fears he helps us face on our pathway through life towards personal empowerment. I have already related the story of the soldiers at Mons during the First World War, which is quite a remarkable appearance when hundreds of people were in severe trauma. It is not often that we have stories of large groups of people being looked after altogether, although there have been many stories of people seeing angels

in the skies above them when an aeroplane is in danger of crashing, and suchlike events. It is more usual for each of us to be 'nudged' by our own angel who intervenes, and therefore protects us, when we are about to face often mortal danger, such as reminding us to check on burning candles, or to take our foot off the car accelerator, or even to miss a plane, which then literally saves our lives. All we need do to constantly enjoy their protection is to be aware they are around and ask them to look after us. It really is as simple as that!

Having an angel companion has helped me out of some dangerous situations, too. Some years ago, close to Christmas, I was driving home through a particular area of the city that has the reputation of being unsafe. The route I took would take me into this area for literally a few metres and usually it was no problem whatsoever. Unfortunately, this day I got stuck at traffic lights behind a large refuse collection unit and in front of a construction lorry. As I mentioned earlier, it's a good idea to clear up your passenger seat so that you can invite your angel to travel along with you in your car for protection. Fortunately for me I had cleared my passenger seat for my angel that day.

As I waited for the traffic lights to change two young boys came running down an alleyway to my left and, with upraised arms, they made for my passenger window as though to smash it. I have always been very fortunate and this sort of incident has never happened to me before, and I remember watching the proceedings as though in slow motion with dread. I could almost hear the intake of breath of those other drivers close by who were looking on. Just centimetres from the window the two young boys came to a startling halt, a look of shock and terror crossed their faces, and they raced back up the alleyway without doing any damage to me or my car. What a relief! I don't know precisely what happened, but I firmly believe my angel manifested something or some person in the passenger seat at that very last moment, hence the boys' looks of shock and terror. Now there's magic for you!

Some people may immediately question, 'If there are angels there to protect us, why do such terrible things happen?' There is no doubt that some horrific situations face individuals and I certainly don't have the answer as to why these things happen. I do believe, though, that we ourselves choose the experiences

in order to learn lessons from them which are specific to our own individual needs. Realizing that we do have the choice in the first place can be helpful. Otherwise, what will we be but 'victims' and we will never learn anything from that experience. As one of my Angel Inspiration messages states: *'Those who walk with angels learn to soar above the clouds.'* So there will be clouds (and mighty thunderstorms for some), but when you are walking with the protection of the angels you can learn to soar above them. That doesn't mean nothing difficult will happen even when you do consciously know your angels are with you. It simply means that with angelic help it will be easier for you to face the difficult times and move onwards and upwards, stronger because you faced your lesson and therefore passed the test.

Using the following rituals for protection will help you ensure that you, your home, your loved ones, your workplace and even your neighbourhood is under divine angelic protection. Do remember, however, that each of us does have to learn our own lessons so we may have to face some difficult crises in order to grow. The angels cannot, and will not, force us to do

anything, they can only suggest the right course of action to us. Let's say you care for someone who is drinking and driving and refuses to stop doing so. You can, of course, use the rituals below on his or her behalf. However, the lesson this person needs to learn may be to face the consequences of drinking and driving. With angelic protection that person may have an accident while under the influence and therefore have to 'face the consequences' or 'learn the lesson', but with the angels' help there may be a 'miraculous escape' for anyone else involved who perhaps only has to learn about miracles.

All you need to do to enjoy the protection of angels is to be aware they are around and ask them to look after you.

Rituals for Angelic Protection

✦ Whenever you are facing a problem, or even travelling down a dark road at night, say:

Angel Magic

The Angel of Divine Protection goes before me and prepares my way.

✦ When you wish you could just disappear because there is a group of what seems like unsavoury characters approaching, immediately imagine that the archangel Michael, complete with his sword, is with you, as well as your own angel. Also, you can imagine that your angels are shielding you with their wings. You will find no one on the street even seems to notice you are there when you have this power of protection.

✦ Each of us has our own lessons to learn and it is difficult when we see our loved ones facing problems. We cannot and should not do their lessons for them. But we can encourage them to ask for angelic guidance and protection for themselves. Also, we can give a helping hand by saying:

The Angel of Divine Protection goes before ___ [name] and prepares his/her way.

✦ When I am driving, especially on long journeys, I always ask the Angel of Divine Protection to be with me, and I also wrap the car around with an aura of angelic protection. I see it in my mind's eye as a white or gold glow covering the car so that no one ever touches me. Thankfully, I have been driving for over 30 years without even a tip from someone else's vehicle. I also carry a sticker with an angelic message on the window of my car. Currently it says *'Never drive faster than your angel can fly,'* and I also have one that reads *'Protected by angels'*. The first reminds me to drive sensibly and the second, I am convinced, frightens away would-be thieves!

Rituals for Protecting Your Home and Workplace from Negative Energies

When you work in an environment such as an office, factory or school there is no doubt that everyone's changing energies can affect each other adversely, especially when there is some sort of dispute going on. It is the same in a family situation, too,

where there are several people all going through difficult times and taking it out on each other! The important thing to realize is that, while your own words may not have the power to help change the negative energies, with your angels' help there are many little ways you can make the difference.

Bullying is quite rampant in some workplaces, especially where stress can be a key factor every day. While there may be legislative backing for you, it isn't easy to put up with constant and niggling harassment or even just plain non co-operation from colleagues or employers/employees. Again, with angelic intervention we can bring magic into a stale, unhelpful and even aggressive situation. If you feel threatened or bullied, say *'The Angel of Divine Protection goes before me and prepares my way.'*

Remember that everywhere you go you are with your angel, and so is everyone else, despite the fact that they may not realize it! Here are some simple ways to create harmony in your home and your workplace.

✦ Ask your angel to speak to the other person's angel in order to bring understanding and harmony into the situation. Keep your request simple, just as though you were talking to a friend, by saying something like: *'Could you please ask ___'s [name] angel to see my side of the situation,'* or *'Could you please bring extra love into the house/workplace today so that we can all co-operate with each other.'* As you meet one another, think in your mind, *'The light within me salutes the light within you',* and by doing so you will be much more enlightened in your approach to one another.

◆ I find it helps a lot if you realize that when another person is in your company, whatever you think of them, they also have an angel in their presence. Just imagine what it would be like if we could each see the other person's angel. How our attitude would change from belligerence to compassion! Now, just once, imagine you can see that person's angel and speak to the angel, rather than to the person. In that way you will more easily choose words which will create harmony rather than disharmony. Yes, thinking about it can be difficult, but try it anyway and you may be amazed at the outcome. In my own experience, when I have had 'problem relationships', I have often managed to bring about harmony

by having a conversation in my mind with the other person's angel when I am in their company. So, while I am talking out loud with the person, I am communicating silently with their angel.

✦ Write a letter to the other person's angel, asking that the situation be cleared up between you both with understanding and compassion. Then it is up to the other person's angel to do the explaining, but you must also be open to making peace. Keep the letter simple. The angels know our intent, and they are only waiting for us to intercede with love. If I was having what I call a 'growth opportunity' (in other words, a problem!) with someone, I would write something like this: *'Dear John's angel, Please help us both to find a way to understand the anger between us and give us extra love so that we can forgive each other. Thank you very much.'*

✦ When you just need extra help in a situation, say *'The Angel of Divine Love is working through me right now in order to bring about the perfect outcome in this situation.'* The 'perfect outcome' is the right outcome. It can mean a break up if

your relationship is meant to break up, or that you resign from your job, if that is what you are meant to do. It will not cause these things to happen unless they are the 'perfect outcome' for you.

Always remember we can never force anyone to change, no matter how hard we try. Transformation must come from within, but with an angel's help we can offer an opportunity for change to the people we share our world with, through showering angelic love on them. It is up to them to accept it or discard it. The main reasons for uncertainty and insecurity in society are based on a lack of love, which is just another term for fear. Once we share the loving nature of our angels, we can help to protect our home, and in turn our village, our country and our planet from negative energies.

Rituals for Protecting Your Neighbourhood

You can not only ensure that your home is under angelic protection, you can also expand it to the neighbours' property. Try the following rituals whether you are in the house itself or thousands of miles away.

Imagine you are getting a bird's eye view of your home, your gardens, the footpath, your neighbours on either side ... See it in as much clear detail as possible. There are three separate rituals you can try:

1. Imagine that a funnel of bright light is coming down from the heavens and it is covering the entire scenario. This is the light of angelic protection and, no matter what is happening in other areas around you, this section of your neighbourhood is now protected.

2. Imagine there are four angels, one placed at the north, one at the south, one at the east, one at the west, each of them holding a corner of a lightly woven cloth. This cloth is

completely covering the scenario that you have seen in your mind's eye. Imagine the cloth being spun gold, or white, or indigo.

3. Imagine the archangel Michael carrying his sword as he stands outside your home/car/office protecting it.

✦ Here is another quick ritual to help you protect your neighbourhood:

Find in your own mind the tallest building in your neighbourhood, which can often be the spire of a church, but it can be any edifice. Now in your mind's eye see an angel, or a group of angels, sitting on the top of this place. From the area of the angel's heart there shines a brilliant golden light. The light grows bigger and bigger as it expands with the love that your angel is showing you. It spreads out and covers the neighbouring buildings and roadways, then it grows larger and spreads out again, covering a wider area, including your own home. The brilliant light now covers the roads, the cars, the front gardens, the rear gardens and the houses. Allow it to grow as big as you need it to be until you

feel very much protected in your neighbourhood. You may have to carry out this on a nightly basis for a while if you live in an area where petty crime is regular, but you should soon discover that the crime rate drops rather dramatically and surprisingly!

✦ In the following visualization exercise you can help to shower love on your neighbourhood and so keep it safe and 'enlightened'.

Visualization Exercise: Protecting Your Neighbourhood

By now you should automatically be enjoying these exercises in a quiet, comfortable place with no disturbances for at least 30 minutes. It's easiest if you record the script first onto an audio tape, or else if you are doing it in a group situation have one person read it out. Make sure you are sitting comfortably and play some gentle background music if you wish. Remember we have two lungs, so use them both as you breathe in and out and you will find it easier to enter a relaxed state.

Start off by reminding yourself that you are safely connected to the Earth by the little magnets on the soles of your feet. As you begin to breathe in, it is as though a gentle blue light is coming up from the earth below and moving up into the soles of your feet, filling them all the way to your toes and across to your ankles. As you breathe out, any tiredness in your feet disappears, and as you breathe in again the blue light slowly and gently travels up your lower legs and into your knees. Now the old, stale energy disappears as you breathe out, and now as you breathe in again the blue energy moves upwards into your thighs and hips. Gently releasing your breath and with it any negative energy, you breathe in deeply again and now the blue light moves into your lower torso. Breathing out and in again, the blue light moves into your upper torso and, as you breathe out, the negative or tired energy is released. Now as you breathe in, the blue light moves into your spine and it is as though your entire backbone is cleansed and healed as the blue light gently climbs upwards and heals each vertebrae. Now the old stale energy disappears as you breathe out, and as you breathe in

again the blue light moves into your shoulders, helping you to release any burdens that you are carrying, and it moves down into your upper arms, your elbows, your lower arms and into your hands. All the while that you breathe in you are drawing in blue healing light, and all the while that you breathe out you are exhaling tired, negative energy.

Now as you breathe in, the energy is moving into your neck and your throat, and now it is entering your head. It is moving around your jaw line, into your mouth, into your ears and up to your cheekbones. It is moving into your nose and your eyes, your forehead, under your scalp and into your hair. Now it has reached the top of your head and, as you breathe out any stale energy from before, you now realize that you are filled with pure blue healing light. It is a wonderful feeling to know that you are connected with healing energy just by thinking about it. The blue healing energy goes to any place in your body which requires healing. Enjoy the feeling of any energy blocks being gently dissolved. You can feel the healthy flow of energy moving all through your body.

Imagine now that you are standing on a small hill close to where you live. As you look around you, you can see the familiar neighbourhood. Take a good look and you will quickly recognize some landmarks. Perhaps you can even see your own home from this vantage point.

Now you realize that your angel is beside you, looking at the same vista. You know that, together, you can help to clear away any darkness in your neighbourhood brought about by sadness and misunderstanding, by fear and lack of love. You can feel your angel's closeness and the warmth of love between you. As you turn to look at each other your angel opens its wings and enfolds you in love. Now your feet are leaving the ground and you can feel yourself safely move upwards into the air. Your angel's wings are carrying you. You feel happy and safe, with a bubbling sense of happy anticipation growing inside.

You feel the gentle rush of air around your face and hair as you move across the landscape and higher into the air. Now you and your angel are above the familiar buildings and close to your home. You are now flying above the roof of your home. You

find that in your hands is a large container of silver angel confetti. You and your angel begin to shower it down on your home. This angel confetti acts like magic and everywhere it falls it lightens up any darkness. It is shining in the street, and it is lighting up the trees and the gardens.

Now, as you continue to shower this angelic confetti below you, you can see people coming out of their homes and offices and looking about them in amazement at the light. Whereas once they may have felt separate from each other, now they greet one another joyfully and you can see them smiling and laughing and sharing friendship. Some of these people look upwards towards the light and their faces are shining with happiness.

You continue on your journey through the skies and come to another place where there is the darkness of misunderstanding and fear. Perhaps you know this place intimately, or perhaps you have just heard that it is going through difficult times. You may not even know how to pronounce its name, but your angel will understand that you want to go there. Once more you are flying with your angel above the buildings. You and your *companion shower the silver angel confetti down on this place. People, perhaps strangers, come out to see the light which is magically dissolving the darkness. There may be some who extend the hand of friendship to their neighbour for the first time and you see how joyful they are as their familiar surroundings are magically transformed by the angelic light.*

There is no hurry and there is an unending supply of angel confetti. You and your companion can travel to as many places as you wish and return home when it feels right for you. (Give as much time as you wish for this.)

You feel happy and fulfilled as you now begin to make your journey home. Your angel reminds you that you can go on this journey together whenever you feel a lack of love in your home or your neighbourhood, or even further afield. But for now you find yourself standing on the hilltop where you began this journey and it is time to come back.

And now I want you to take a deep breath and as you breathe in and out, once more you can feel the ground beneath your feet. And now as you breathe in and out again, you can feel your

*fingertips and your toes. And now as you breathe in and out, it
is time to open your eyes, and you do so, coming back into this
room, feeling relaxed, refreshed and much better than before.*

Chapter 8

The Angels of Children

It seems we all know about angels, even as tiny beings newly-born. If you have ever looked into the eyes of a newborn baby you may have been quite startled as to what you saw. It's often very obvious that in the soul of babies there is a wealth of knowledge which far surpasses our own; it's as though the baby looks into our soul and says 'I know', despite the fact it cannot speak or fend for itself. Perhaps that strong feeling is our own spirit responding as though recognizing a friend from the past. Usually, however, as the infant develops physically the

special unspoken knowledge drifts into the ether, and any formal education, based on logical left brain development rather than intuitive right brain 'knowing', will immediately erase any vestiges that remain! I remember my own niece, before she had attended school, saying to me shyly, 'Remember the last time we were here? It wasn't like this at all, was it?' How I wish I'd had a tape recorder to keep a record of our conversation!

Children do know about angels. I certainly did, and in recent years I have met countless children who talk freely of their daily experiences even though their parents may not know about them. Fortunately, the current climate encourages such admissions, so there is no need for these youngsters to feel in any way 'left out' when they do open up. You may be pleasantly surprised to discover just how much your child knows about angels already! Why not bring up the subject today?

There is a lovely true story related by American journalist George Howe Colt which tells that when his wife was having a difficult pregnancy they developed a kinship with some pigeons whose chicks were nestled precariously on their window-ledge high above street level in New York City. They believed that if the chicks survived the apparent daily dangers so, too, would their promised baby girl. Fortunately, they all managed to survive through some rather difficult times as the months went by. Some years later, their daughter who was now six years old, suddenly explained to her father that angels don't look like people. She explained that they come to Earth in a form that humans won't object to. 'In New York', she said, 'they come as pigeons.'

Encourage the children you know to bring their angels into their lives. Explain how their angels can protect them and help them as well as the people they love. Children feel omnipotent from an early age; they know they have the power to create the life they desire, and often take on the silent burden of guilt should disaster touch those they love through accident, divorce, and so on. Apart from their feeling of impotence in such instances, they often feel incapable of expressing their hurt, they are convinced no one will listen to them, and they often feel very much alone. By explaining that their angel is with them at all times and practising some of the following rituals,

you can help them accept what they cannot change and bring about change when they can.

Whether or not you are a parent, enjoy the following rituals. After all, we each have our own 'Inner Child'!

Encourage the children you know to bring their angels into their lives.

Rituals for Bringing Angels into Children's Lives

✦ The following ritual is based on an ancient Chinese custom. Explain that the birds of the air act as the angels' messengers. When we have problems that seem too difficult to solve, take some cooked rice or breadcrumbs, and mentally put your requests into these small particles of food. Leave the food out for the birds and they will carry your messages up to God on behalf of you and your angels.

✦ If you have a small patch of garden, set aside a little place which is especially for your child's angel. (Where there is no

garden, use a plant pot). Allow your child to sow and plant this special garden. Pick some angel pictures or figurines which can be 'planted' in this space. Every day encourage your child to tend this special place.

✦ Every morning encourage the use of the Angel Inspiration Cards as shown in Chapter 3. If your child has a particular problem that needs extra help, use the card messages whenever the situation requires it.

✦ Play a daily game of 'I know my angel loves me because ... ' and encourage different answers, such as '... because I have you', '... because I'm always safe', and so forth. Try to think up five different answers each time you play the game.

✦ Every now and again lay an extra place at your table for an angel and invite it to join you for mealtime. By doing so, you will automatically bring peace and harmony into your family life.

✦ Encourage your child to be alert to angelic presence and angelic presents! Look out for the unexpected appearing in unusual places, such as a white feather, a silver coin, a flower, and so on.

+ Especially in cases of bullying, remember the saying *'The Angel of Divine Protection goes before me and prepares my way.'* Most children are very visual so talk about archangel Michael and his sword. Ask your child what their Angel of Divine Protection would look like in order to bring it into reality for them.

+ At school your child can call on special angels to help in class such as the Angel of Divine Understanding or the Angel of Knowing, especially where tests are concerned (though, of course, your child has to have done the work first in order to pass!). These angels can help to quell panic and recall the required knowledge. As always, when talking to angels keep the language informal and friendly, such as: *'Angel of Divine Understanding, please help me to remember the work I've done so that I can have the perfect outcome in this examination.'*

+ Encourage your child to imagine a shield is protecting them from any negative influences approaching them, and imagine that their angel is standing behind them at all times.

✦ Practise standing still and imagining white light coming down from heaven and enveloping you both from head to toe in protective angelic light.

Rituals for when You are Apart

Should you have to be away from your children for any period of time, you can practise some rituals to ensure their welfare and safety. Do remember that your thoughts can create reality, so as you think of them, imagine good things happening to all those you love, with lots of laughter and joy vibrating outwards.

✦ Ask your angel to speak to your child's angel and send them love and protection.

✦ You can also ask the angel Afriel, the guardian of young life, to take special care of your children when you are apart. Say: *Angel Afriel, who looks after young children, I assign my child ___ [name] into your care. I ask that you use Divine Light to shine on her/him, and that you enfold her/him in your wings with love.*

✦ When you have to be apart for long periods, carry a photograph of your little one and light a candle close to it should you ever feel uneasy. As you do so, ask your angel to protect and guard your child.

Visualization Exercise: A Ritual for Children

The veracity of the power of suggestion has been proven for many years and by using visualization techniques you can help to encourage children to feel safe and secure by understanding that their angel is looking after them. These visualization exercises can also help children to let go of fears by inviting their angels to be with them when they face any obstacles.

You can read this out when they are in bed, or record it onto a tape and play it for them. Don't worry if they go to sleep during the exercise – their spirit is still awake even though their physical body and ego is sleeping. You know your child best, so use the following as a blueprint and change the content whenever and wherever you feel it necessary depending on their age, and their likes and dislikes.

Just make sure that you take your time when you are giving this visualization (allow about 12–15 minutes). The result will be happy, content children so it's worth the effort!

The script goes as follows:

Imagine that you're a tree. Imagine your feet are the roots of this tree and feel them pushing into the soil below. How cosy and safe you feel, rooted to the ground. Now you can imagine a warm glow rising up from your feet. Imagine it as a lovely orange glow as it moves up into your legs, and now it's in your knees, and now it's in your hips. Now you can feel that lovely orange glow moving into your body and down your arms and up into your head. It's lovely being a tree! Your arms are the branches and your head is the top of the tree. You can feel the wind gently moving through the branches and you can see the birds flying by.

Now, let's go on an adventure in your mind. You are going for a walk in a lovely garden. You can see lots of flowers. There are red flowers and orange flowers; there are yellow flowers and

green plants. There are blue flowers and purple flowers and white flowers. They are so pretty you love looking at them. Now you see someone coming towards you. You are very happy to know that it is your angel. Your angel comes closer and you sit down together. You feel warm and comfortable as you feel its wings around you.

Now your angel tells what its name is. [Pause] Your angel tells you that it loves you and it will always be with you because it is its job to be with you and give you help when you ask for it. You must remember to ask for help and it will always be there.

Are you ready to receive a special gift? This is a gift from your angel to remind you that it is always there and how much it loves you. Whenever you need extra help remember this gift and it will remind you of how you met today. Remember that if ever you need extra help you just have to call on your angel.

And now it's time to come back to your warm, comfy bed and remember all the things you saw on your adventure. So breathe in deeply and, as you breathe out, you can once more feel your feet and your hands. And breathe in deeply again and, as you

breathe out, you can once more feel your body from the top of
your head to the tips of your toes. And now, as you breathe in
and out again, you know it is time to open your eyes and return
to this room.

Share with your child what the experience was like and, if
the name given was something as simple as 'John' or 'Mary',
don't be disappointed. Angels want to be friends with their
charges, and what better way to be accepted as everyday
friends than to have an everyday name? Depending on what
the gift is, perhaps you could either buy it, have your child
make it, or even simply draw it and hang it up on the bed-
room wall. In this way the angel's presence will be all the
stronger for your child. It is also important to know that
the gift symbolizes something that the child needs in their
life right now. What could it mean? You could discuss it
together and try out various possibilities.

As you and your child become more familiar with the
magic of enjoying such visualizations, you may be told

things which have so far remained a secret, such as their fear of bullying at school, or an unspoken terror that you might abandon them because you were in a bad mood one day. This is one way that the angels work magic – it doesn't have to be with shooting stars and beams of white light! All children need love, understanding and support and with the angels' help you can bring that long-term magic into their lives so that they can grow into healthy, secure adults.

A Final Word

It is important to understand that angels are here for us all every second of every hour of every day. They are here to help us get that little bit closer to heaven, but it is your responsibility to invite them into your life. There is no limit to their love and support, and no payment is required. It is nice to say 'thank you' to them every now and again, and you can return the compliment of their love by mentioning to others how angels bring magic into your life on a daily basis.

The Angels of Children

I hope you have enjoyed this book and that it has helped you bring that special ingredient, angel magic, into your everyday life.

Angel magic is within everyone's grasp, so let's all share it.

Further Information

Recommended Reading

Here are some books you might like to read:

Rosemary Altea, *The Eagle and the Rose* (Rider Books, 2001)

William Barrett, *Deathbed Visions* (Aquarian, 1986)

Pierre Jovanovic, *Inquiry into the Existence of Angels* (M. Evans & Company, 1995)

Eileen Elias Freeman, *Angelic Healing* (Warner Books, 1995)

Further Information

_____, *Touched by Angels* (Warner Books, 1994)

The Findhorn Community, *The Findhorn Garden*
(The Findhorn Press, 1988)

Dr John C. Lilly, *The Scientist* (Ronin Publishing, 1988)

Gitta Mallasz, *Talking with Angels* (Daimon Books, 1992)

Raymond Moody, *The Light Beyond* (Bantam Books, 1988)

___, *Life After Life* (Rider Books, 2001)

___, *Reflections on Life After Life* (Bantam Books, 1977)

Dr Melvin Morse (with Paul Perry), *Closer to the Light*, (Bantam
Books, 1991)

Margaret Neylon, *Open Your Heart to Angel Love* (Angelgate
Publishing, 1996)

Catherine Ponder, *The Prospering Power of Love* (DeVorss & Co,
1966)

Cherie Sutherland, *Children of the Light* (Souvenir Press Ltd,
1996)

____, *In the Company of Angels* (Gateway, 2001)

Edmond Bordeaux Szekely, *The Gospel of the Essenes*
(C. W. Daniel Co Ltd, 1976)

Terry Lynn Taylor, *Creating With Angels* (H. J. Kramer Inc, 1993)

About the Author

If you have enjoyed this book you may wish to know that the following items are also available from Margaret Neylon at the address opposite:

Guided visualizations on cassette as follows:

'Talking With Angels'

'Healing With Angels'

'Angel Love'

'Angel Magic'

Angel Inspiration Cards (set of 40 'angelic messages')

Further Information

Margaret Neylon is available to give seminars and workshops, and can be contacted at:

'Angelgate',
Virginia,
County Cavan,
Ireland.

Or you can contact her directly by email:
angelgate@eircom.net

Rosemary Ellen Guiley

An Angel in Your Pocket

They don't wear wings, they don't live on clouds, but they do come into our lives. Angels are more than figments of our imagination – they are real and have changed the lives of many ordinary people.

Throughout history artists have painted them, poets have written about them, and films have portrayed them. This beautiful gift book looks at the history of angels and how they have been depicted throughout history. It answers many questions, such as `who are they? what are they? and where do they come from?'

Rosemary Ellen Guiley

A Miracle in Your Pocket

How to bring miracles into your daily life

Discover how anyone can bring Miracles into their daily life with this inspirational gift book.

Drawing on both famous miracles from history and modern anecdotal accounts for illustration. And it will offer the readers inspirational and practical advice for bringing `miracle consciousness' into their own daily lives. Miracles are not just the stuff of exalted saints and holy ones, but the products of a creative power we all have the ability to access.

Nigel Pennick

Thorsons Way of Natural Magic

Following on from First Directions .. this new series provides a more in-depth, sophisticated introduction. A grounded and authoritative look at magic from an established author that provides simple but powerful practical techniques that anyone can use to bring more magic into their everyday lives.

Richard Lawrence

Little Book of Karma

The secret of success in every aspect of your life

Who needs The Little Book of Calm – karma is where it's at!
Karma determines everything from the evolution of the universe to the smallest details of your life. Make this little book
your companion, guiding you to fulfilment and success.

Dr Richard Lawrence

Magic of Healing

Heal yourself and others with this unique combination of ancient yoga practices and the latest spiritual techniques

Healing is a way of transferring natural energies to others, both to maintain a sense of well being and to heal. It is something we all have the ability to do and if we practise the techniques in this book anyone can bring about remarkable results.

Fiona Horne

Seven Days to a Magickal New You

Fiona Horne is a Witch with Attitude – young, beautiful and extremely funky. Here she shares the secrets of her craftwith this week-long guide to releasing your own inner witch!

This enchanting guide takes you day-by-day on a week-long journey of magickal transformation. With each day ruled by a different planet, this little book is packed with fun and practical suggestions, from breakfast picnics to decorating your own altar. Includes easy and inspiring ways to bring more magick into your life and enhance your feelgood factor, including day by day rituals, simple chakra work, how to make elixirs and other potions.

Make
www.thorsonselement.com
your online sanctuary

www.thorsonselement.com

thorsons
element